A Memoir

EVOLUTION
OF A
WILD
HEART

AN ARTIST JOURNEY
INTO NATURE

BY

JOANNE HELFERT SULLAM

DayDreams Studio Press

Published and distributed by: Daydreams Studio Press

PO Box 740

Saugerties, NY 12477

daydreamsstudios@gmail.com

Library of Congress Control Number: 2022909017

1st edition

Publisher's Cataloging-in-Publication data

Names: Sullam, JoAnne Helfert, author.

Title: Evolution of a Wild Heart / JoAnne Helfert Sullam.

Description: Saugerties NY: Daydreams Studio Press, 2022.

Identifiers: LCCN: 2022909017 | ISBN: 979-8-9863177-0-0

Subjects: LCSH Sullam, JoAnne Helfert. | Artists--Biography. | Women--Biography. | Nature. | Animals in art. | BISAC BIOGRAPHY & AUTOBIOGRAPHY / Personal Memoirs | BIOGRAPHY & AUTOBIOGRAPHY / Artists, Architects, Photographers | BIOGRAPHY & AUTOBIOGRAPHY / Environmentalists & Naturalists

Classification: LCC N6537 .S85 2022 | DDC 700.92--dc23

In writing this book I've focused on the people and animals and things that had the biggest impact on my emotional and artistic evolution. I have, for privacy reasons, left out and changed some of the names in this book. This is my story as I recall it.

This book is dedicated to my girls,

Melissa and Julianne,

And to all my wild children—

A depth of gratitude for helping me feel the light of love.

TABLE OF CONTENTS

Evolution: The process of natural selection. The change in characteristics of a life-form that takes a great amount of precious time to happen.

Evolution was now mine to claim.

I was a seed of nature, then a caterpillar of modern life.

I wasn't born to be a bowhead whale with a lifespan of two hundred years and a vast sea to explore.

Yet, I was grateful because I'd already had more than the mayfly who only lives for one small, single day. I would be somewhere in the middle of the shortest and longest life on earth. I was a human life, with a question mark of time.

I realized that whatever time I had, I should use it well. To do that, I would need to wrap myself in my own darkness and feel the pain and beauty of change.

Inside a chrysalis, I exposed the lies I was told—and that I told myself.

It was in that darkness, that loneliness, that fear that I encountered growth.

When I climbed out to dry my wings in contemplation of flight, I discovered a gift of lightness and left my fears and sorrows behind for laugher and joy evolving into a butterfly—the best version of myself.

CHAPTER 1:

IN A NUTSHELL

I grew up in a ghetto. Elvis Presley sung a tale about how tragic and violent it was. He was right—it was a sad and dangerous place. His song "In the Ghetto" lasted two minutes and fifty-eight seconds. My experience in that Brooklyn ghetto lasted over fourteen years. When I left, I did so with a black garbage bag of clothes and post-traumatic stress disorder.

I had gone to the same Catholic school as my father. We studied religion and Latin and I prayed a lot. Being dyslexic, learning disabled, and having a speech impediment, crooked teeth and a bad haircut, among other things, made me a target for bullying. It left me lonely and friendless. My Italian grandmother gave me that bad bowl haircut and told me I was too skinny. I was—and often told if I stood sideways, I'd disappear. And in a way I did. The second oldest of four children, I was the elder middle child. The forgotten one. My older sister was two years older. My younger sister was nine years younger, my brother ten years.

When I failed second grade, and no one could help me read or spell properly, I took matters into my own hands and taught myself to read at home, where I discovered a newfound love of books and the art of storytelling.

At nine I started a journal in my black-and-white notebook. I wrote in code—made up stories that only I knew what they meant. I did this because I had no privacy and knew that my mother would look at it but never understand it. Bad spelling, messy handwriting, and a made-up story would surely confuse my mom to my true feelings.

After moving, when people would inquire where I was from, I would feel embarrassed, look away, and avoid answering by asking them a question or changing the subject.

In suburbia, at fifteen, I did a drawing of a dog. It was a boxer from an ad I'd seen in the *TV Guide* my father read. The ad said, *Could you draw this?* The drawing I did was on a scrap of paper with a #2 pencil and looked just like the one in the ad. *Yes!* I could draw that.

Then my five-year-old brother scribbled over it with a green crayon. When I saw what he did, I snapped.

"What did you do!" I screeched, demanding an answer in the small kitchen of our two-bedroom basement apartment. He looked up, and I cannot recall what he said; I only remember the look in his eyes.

I learned three things that day.

One, that I hurt my little brother's feelings and would hold on to the guilt and self-loathing for yelling at him. I loved him, so I committed to being a better sister to my siblings.

Two, that I cared about that stupid little drawing.

Three, that I could draw.

But it was a passing curiosity and not in my plans for what I wanted to be when I grew up. I had planned on being a veterinarian and a superhero at five. That changed to a social worker at fifteen. At sixteen, I decided to join the Red Cross or Peace Corps, to travel and see the world. Helping people and animals was always important to me.

My father loved animals and allowed me to have them, even though my mother hated them. But we all feared the rats and hated the roaches that invaded our home.

My dad once bought me an alligator as a pet.

Other pets I had growing up were hamsters, guppies, a dog I named Candy that I rescued from the streets of the ghetto, as well as a goose named Pete and a white rabbit named Sam that were supposed to be dinner.

There were no art classes or creative activities in Catholic school, nor art supplies at home. I never took art in high school, instead I took drama and swimming. Then I dropped out of high school at seventeen. That was after I came home and announced I was going to college.

My mother puckered her lips as she did when stressed or angry. My father just left the room. Shocked and confused, I said, "What?" It was like I'd announced I was pregnant.

My mother shook her head and said, "He knows you'll never go."

"Why? I thought he'd be happy." I swallowed hard to hold back the tears.

"You're not smart enough," she said, then she walked away too.

Proving her right about me, I got pregnant at nineteen—the same age she got pregnant with me. Then married the eighteen-year-old boy who was the father and who I'd dated at fifteen. Shortly after we broke up back then, a fire broke out in our house, and although everyone was okay, I had lost everything but the clothes on my back.

My dog, bird, fish, my hamsters, a guitar, some photos, and my record collection. It taught me that things are just things, and loved ones in your life can be taken from you at any time. It left me always waiting for something bad to happen—and it often did.

Later, proving my parents wrong, I got my GED and *did* go to college at twenty-two. My mother said it was only art school and not a real college.

"Mom, I still have to take all the academic classes, like English, math, and history, *plus art*. It's one of the best schools in the country."

She wasn't convinced.

Being the first one in my family to go to college was historic. My cousin on my mother's Italian family side told me so at another cousin's baby shower. She said she was proud of me, and I teared up and thanked her.

Choosing my major was hard. I went with graphic design because I was told you could get a good job in that field. Plus, I was too afraid to do what I really wanted, which was study fine art write and make films. I loved films as much as art, animals, and books.

Even though I wanted to paint and draw wild animals in college, I instead painted and drew domesticated, nude humans. There were no wildlife art classes, so I taught myself how to paint fur and feathers.

Learning that no one made money being an artist, I needed a job. I had a child to care for, and my husband made minimum wage. He also bought an expensive stereo and car parts as I waitressed on weekends and nights. My two-year-old daughter would sometimes go to school with me on days I went to museums and art galleries on the Lower East Side of Manhattan. My husband never did. But he brought her to the restaurant to eat Greek food while I worked. I loved her so much and loved that everyone was always fussing over her pretty little face and sparkly personality. She was a big part of the reason I finally went to college.

In my second-year photography class we had been given an assignment to do a self-portrait. That's when I saw the truth of me in black and white and ten shades of gray. A truth of lies clear as day caught in my eyes. Something was wrong with me, and I believed I was the only one who saw it.

That self-portrait became the catalyst to unraveling the tangled web of self-hatred woven into my fabric. Yet, it would take years and a long journey to discover and be true to myself.

A journey that would lead to an evolution of the soul that lived in my body and needed to be set free.

CHAPTER 2:

THE SELF-PORTRAIT

Taking the shade off the lamp, putting it on the floor after getting ready, felt ritualistic, as if I was preparing for a ceremony of sorts.

In preparation, I had layered my makeup to set the stage, then blow-dried my hair in the mirror on the wall next to the door in our bedroom.

But there wasn't much space to move around in the small bedroom of the bungalow. The only good thing about the place was that it was only a half block from the beach I loved.

My husband was out with his friends, and my four-year-old daughter, Mellissa, was sleeping in the room next to mine. Alone in the room and quiet in the house I felt free to focus on the self-portrait assignment.

After setting my camera on the tripod in front of the closet, I looked through the lens.

In gauging the height I would need for the shot, I thought about where I would sit and if the angle and distance from where I would sit felt right.

It did, so I took off my shirt, wrapped a towel around my chest, and shut off the overhead light. My only light source would be that bare bulb from the lamp. Blinded by flashes of red from looking at the hundred-watt bulb, I fumbled with the timer on the camera. Then I sat on the edge of the bed to begin.

I listened for the click of the camera—reset, click, reset. I did this over and over until it felt done, each time looking away. Then there was one time at the end of my photoshoot when I actually looked into the camera trusting that I'd tell the truth about myself in the same way that I was always seeking the truth of life, only now I was seeking it of myself. I believed the only way to be a real artist was to be uncomfortably honest.

So I made myself uncomfortable by looking into the lens.

My curiosity as to what I'd discover on the roll of film had filled me with anticipation.

The next day, as I headed to the photography department at school, the roll of film became my only thought in a mind normally filled with clutter. On the way I stopped to say hello to Marven, the gatekeeper of the photography lab. I often showed him my photos. He knew all the photography instructors and helped me and the other students with honest, kind assessments of our works and tips on what each teacher looked for. Marven had long dreadlocks, walked as if he was skating across the room, and always had something witty to say.

I wondered what he would think about the photos I was about to develop.

Saying my goodbyes, I left him and the overhead fluorescent lights with only a faint red light to guide me in the darkroom. My other senses became heightened, then offended by the smell of strong chemicals as I approached my workstation.

There where themes to the assignments we were given in the photography class; depth of field, composition, types of shots like long, medium, close-ups, and so on. Otherwise, besides the specific self-portrait assignment we got to choose our subject matter. I photographed all the things I loved: trees, flowers, water, animals, children. My own child was my favorite subject to photograph. To my delight, my sweet little girl was always ready to pose for me. "Why don't you stand by the tree, honey?" I'd ask while holding my camera. "Okay, Mommy," she'd reply as she ran to the big oak tree, tilted her head, and shrugged. I would snap away as she posed like a professional, then thank her for the effort.

Unbeknownst to Melissa she also modeled as I practiced for my drawing class. I would draw her watching TV, sleeping, and anytime she stood still enough.

Her face became as familiar to my class as mine since she was my most frequent subject. I wanted Melissa to have the cultural and artistic experiences I hadn't been given. So, with some of the students from class, I would sometimes take her gallery-hopping in Manhattan. After we came back from the art museums and shows, she would sit with us in restaurants and listen as we discussed the art we had just seen. She always had her own opinion about it. She was outgoing, social, and articulate—all characteristics I'd hoped to gain myself.

After processing the film, I set out to make a contact sheet. Photography paper was expensive, and I had to be careful not to waste any. Everything in college was expensive and necessary. Consequently, I had to be economical and creative with whatever I bought.

But with very little money to spend on supplies I couldn't compete with the other students on some of the projects. At times it felt stagnating to the creative prosses, yet it taught me how to be resourceful, which led to more creative ways of solving some of my material needs. Even so, there was a downside as it made me think I could never rise above that awful feeling that poverty leaves you with.

It seemed to me, true or not, that the other students had an end-less flow of funds from proud parents. In truth I didn't know anyone's story on how they made it to a private college. Life up to that point was black and white for me. Happy or sad, good or bad. Binary think-ing. He was right, I was wrong. She was wrong, I was right. Fill in the names, the places, and any one or other thing that happened could be turned into a case for black-and-white thinking.

Now everything in black and white also had ten shades of gray. It was the shades of gray that interested me most. Even in painting class I was taught to focus on the tones and values first, not the colors. The colors would have their place in a supporting role to shape composition and form. Besides learning about art, school had opened my eyes to observing and a new way of thinking. Something I had always done, but now it was being refined.

Having layered the negatives over the photo paper, I put them in the developer and watched the white paper submerge in the clear liquid until the images appeared.

After hanging the paper to dry, I stepped outside for some fresh air and a walk.

Back In the darkroom, I was about to face the truth of some of those shades of gray, only this time on developed film.

With a magnifier, I examined the 2x2-inch photos of the strips of six frames that covered the 8x10-inch paper. There were only three im-ages that made it to the precious photo paper. Two were of me looking away. The one that made my stomach flutter was the one of me looking into the lens as I would into the mirror. Something I often avoided.

That's the one, I thought. That was the one I'd bring to class.

The self-portrait felt raw, and I had conflicted feelings about sharing it.

As an artist, this wasn't the first time I was hesitant to share my work. It made me feel exposed—but free. I wanted the freedom of expression and liberation and release of emotions that art offers. Despite this, the sharing comes with a cost of vulnerability and fear of rejection.

My first day I had a drawing class. Our task was to draw our hands. It was all I could do not to run out screaming, "I don't belong here! I'm not a real artist!" That feeling overcame me as I looked around at everybody drawing beautiful Renaissance-style hands. I became more embarrassed by my feeble attempt to draw my shaking hand, then humiliated when we were asked to hang them on the wall for critiquing.

I felt my face flush when the teacher singled out my drawing. I shifted comfortably and sunk down in my seat like I did when I was child being called on to spell words I didn't know how to spell. I expected him to say how horrible my work was and how he couldn't even understand how I got into such a great art school.

But he surprised me when he said mine was a real hand and the drawing was true and not made of preconceived notions of what a perfect hand should be. I thought I was going to faint when he said, "She drew her hand and how she felt about it. That's what I asked of you, not to draw Michelangelo's hand. Now forget everything you learned about drawing in high school and give me something real, like JoAnne did."

The subjects I focused on, like my own shaky hand and now the self-portrait, were the ones I found the most difficult to examine and share.

It was all so frightening. Like becoming a mother. I felt like damaged goods and unworthy of such a precious thing as a child. But when I found out I was pregnant I couldn't imagine life without her. I wanted her to be proud to call me Mom as she grew and learned to walk and talk, and it helped me strive to be a better person and mother.

Then going to college was almost as terrifying as having a child. I was afraid I wasn't smart or talented enough. Then when I got in, I was very subconscious about being slightly older than the other students. I had never taken art in high school and felt like I would never be as good as some of them, maybe even all of them.

Because before I had Melissa, I spent my free time reading, not drawing. No real art, just a doodle here and there, sometimes on napkins or in my journal. Art didn't seem that important to my education or being a mother or getting a good job.

Thinking back to when I was pregnant, I had devoured books like a caterpillar through a leaf. Reading the works of Shakespeare, John Keats, Edgar Allan Poe, and Lovecraft made me hungry for more. Waddling down to the local library, like a home full of treasures.

Propping my swollen feet on the couch, then the book on my big belly, I would read aloud to my unborn child—Emily Dickinson's poetry and Emily Brontë's *Wuthering Heights*. The baby in my belly was too young for Stephen King who I'd been reading for my own bedtime stories since I was twelve.

My early love for gothic horror grew, so did a love of poetry. After the baby was born, in between feeding and diaper changes, I worked though Hemingway and read Virginia Wolf. I loved Hemingway's writing style and wished I could write like that. Reading child sociology books was a bit boring at times, but I felt it would help me be a better mom. While learning how to play chess and trying to beat my husband in the game I got books on chess moves.

Why didn't I become a writer or book editor? Why an artist? Being dyslexic, I could be an artist but never a writer. How could I? I couldn't even spell.

"Why can't you just get a real job and be happy with that?" my husband would often say. Then he only said, "Just get a real job," referring to me wanting a creative work life.

"I don't even know what that means," I'd reply. "You want me to work in an office nine to five?"

I can't recall how he'd answered because I would block it out since the idea was so repulsive to me.

Maybe I should have explained that I had always felt like a caged animal, like the ones I had seen at the Bronx Zoo. One day I went there alone so I could study the wild animals I loved but had only read about or seen on television. This was before the zoo had natural enclosers for all the animals. The tiger was pacing inside a concreate cage with metal bars. A gorilla in a similar cage was laying on his back playing with a leaf, and a monkey looked up though the bars at the sky.

I started to cry and had to leave.

That's how working in an office would have made me feel. But I didn't tell my husband that. Instead, I promised him that art school could be good and I would get a respectable job as a graphic designer. Except I didn't know what I was doing. Maybe I panicked and found art to be an answer. It was one of the quickest decisions I ever made as I would normally labor over every decision, large or small, since I never trusted myself to make the right one. Most times I had let life or other people make the decisions for me.

When my daughter was a year old I went browsing through the adult-learning pamphlet that came in the mail and found a class on pastel painting at night school that looked fun. I was hungry to learn something new, and books weren't enough for me anymore. The pamphlet had made me think about the drawing I did of the dog. Also, the sunset had always made me wish I could paint, to capture it and take it home and hang it on the wall. I remember being on the beach at sixteen and watching the sunset, forgetting all my problems and sadness and anxiety that melted down with the pink-and-orange glow of the sun.

Then in an adult-education class I met a teacher who helped me prepare for my GED test; she knew me without even knowing me. She was the first teacher who could walk me through the landmines of my learning disability and teach me how to work around them. She was responsible for my good score on the test, not me. I cannot recall her name, only that she seemed to "get me" in a world where no one else did. The gifts of strangers. She was one of those people who was always smiling.

"You can do this," she would say. That high score on the GED test surprised me. She said, "That's fantastic! What do you want to do now?"

"Well, I did want to go to college."

"What would you study? What do you like to do?"

I showed her my pastel paintings.

"I like art. And I even sold one of my paintings for a hundred dollars. It was a heron in a marsh."

"Then you should apply to the School of Visual Arts. It's the best in the country right now and right in Manhattan."

My mind and nerves reeled with excitement and fear.

I'll never forget what she said as my mind wandered to what my family would think and how I could afford it.

"Always start at the top. What's the worst that could happen? They say no and you try someplace else till you get where you wanna go."

But was this *really* where I wanted to go? I was unsure.

She pushed me on that train and helped me fill out the applications. If it was left up to me, I would still be standing on the platform wondering how I could give my child a good life. She then sent all the applications to the best art schools in New York. She didn't know me at all, but somehow she knew me well. Better than I knew myself.

CHAPTER 3:

CHUGGING TRAINS AND MYSTIFYING MICE

I t took me over an hour to get to school every day, most of it on trains. It gave me time to think or work. I preferred working. But the long ride to and from the city, twice a day, made it hard not to think. It was the sounds of clicking and the hard rocking of the train, mixed with the carcinogenic smell of sluggish air from the subways, that would often trigger a dive into my past.

Most of my memories were ugly and messy. They were the ones I'd passed over as not to trigger some horrid dream. It was better to gloss over those and examine something more manageable.

Getting off the train and walking the corridor at the end of the platform, I spotted a mouse scurrying away and recalled a happy moment from childhood. My heart longed for that joyful, confident, curious, strong-willed child with an inherited love of the natural.

I considered it to be my epigenetic link.

It was the night before Christmas at the sweet age of four, cocooned in my naïveté before the discovery of the hardness of the world. I was in the living room with my dad while he decorated our Christmas tree. The tree that year was perfect. It was wide and tall and full of life, carrying with it a strong smell of pine. Its top branches that had once reached for the sun were now hitting the celling. I looked up at my father putting the finishing touches of angel hair and tinsel over the large glowing lights of red, green, blue, and white. The antique embellished German Christmas ornaments, left behind by family members long gone, hung fragile and worn from years of use and weighed downed the edges of the branches.

I sat content on the floor under the tree.

Looking up at my dad I noted his smile. Was he smiling at the tree and perhaps a joyful memory of his own childhood? I looked down to the tattered Christmas book on my lap. In that book was an illustration of a festive room with a colorful Christmas tree and Santa Claus. The colors were vibrant and fed the artist that I would grow to be. But it was the other part of me, the nature lover in my heart, that set its attention on a small gray mouse with black glossy eyes drawn within the pages. I can't recall where he was in the scene, only that he was part of an idyllic Christmas, just like in my home.

Next to me and under the tree, the oversized Lionel train set from my father's childhood chugged around a winter scene. As it came around to me again, and the small gateman came out of his little house, I cheered with delight.

I loved playing with that train set—turning it on and off, going backward and forward—and at that moment was thinking how much the scene matched the one in the book. Then, as if on cue, a small gray mouse dashed out of the hole chewed away in the molding next to the tree. Right before the train came around to me, he ran under the tree, across the train tracks, and across my lap, disappearing on the other side of the room into the open closet, and I imagined right back into the book. That little mouse was part of our home and had come from some unknown, wild place. I thought he had come there to share Christmas with us. He had made a fairy-tale moment for me where anything was possible and Santa was still real. I trusted this would be my life, just like the happy, magical story in the book. I hadn't been taught yet that wild mice in the house were something to loathe or learned to loathe myself just for being me. I'm sure if my mother was in the room, she would have screamed. I would learn this fear of mice from her when she yelled and jumped on a chair like a cartoon woman in a *Tom and Jerry* episode. It made me laugh. I was with my dad later that spring when I found a dead mouse in the yard. I was curious to examine it and picked it up, and in the excitement of my discovery my dad suggested I show it to my mom. Knowing what her reaction would be, my father wasn't far behind as I ran to the kitchen to show her. He laughed as my mother screamed and jumped on the chair, telling me to take it away. I didn't understand.

My thoughts came back around to the self-portrait and school.

When I came home, and before I was to present the photo in class, I figured I should show it to Howard. He would be my gauge. Could he see what I saw? When I went home my husband had a little all-black puppy that was found on the parkway. It was more than I wanted to take on at the moment, but it was one thing I had loved my husband for, and we shared a soft spot for unwanted pets and often took them in.

We played with the new puppy, then I showed him the photo.

Howard looked at the photo and at me, like he was confirming who it was. Then he told me he wanted to put one in his toolbox at work.

"Okay, I'll make one for you," I said, flattered but suspicious. I wondered if he was sparked by my looks or the inside of me. Which part did he really love?

After we got married Howard seemed to love demoralizing wife jokes. He would make me the punch line. He was a big fan of Rodney Dangerfield, the king of wife jokes. He made me laugh even when he was making fun of me.

Howard said I looked pretty, but I knew better than to think I was attractive; I knew who I really was—the ugly duckling who never became a swan.

There would be so many things I would discover, some of which I would have to unlearn. I couldn't understand why Howard, after the baby, would prefer to spend his time out instead of at home or why I'd had to beg for him to spend time with me and our daughter when he had given it so freely, so completely when we dated.

Like me, Howard loved animals, but did he actually love *me*? What was I missing? What was it about this life that I was attracted to? How had I found my way to art school with a child and a husband while barely making ends meet? As I walked to class with the self-portrait in my hands these were the questions that ran through my mind.

CHAPTER 4

THE UGLY DUCKLING

Working on a drawing assignment at the drafting table, I looked up at the fancy-tailed pigeon sitting on the windowsill. While I listened to it coo in the afternoon light, it brought me back to a little girl I didn't know anymore and was trying to understand. One who had left me feeling like I was the ugly duckling. As I closed my eyes, all I could see was her. Although I knew it was me, I had grown distant from that girl who often stood alone and felt lonely. I remember being in the small courtyard during recess in second grade. I was wearing a Peter Pan shirt and a green plaid wool uniform with our school's name embroidered on it. The Buster Brown-like, hand-me-down shoes barely held together. I hated shoes and would kick them off as soon as I was allowed to. My feet got wet when it rained or snowed, and the shoes were either too tight or too big.

That precise memory of the schoolyard stood out as it was a confirmation of my loneliness and love of animals. Now, at the age of twenty-two, a big part of me still felt like a lonely little girl.

I would watch the pigeons flutter away from my classmates as they played in the small courtyard shrouded by brick. Everyone in class ran around as if I were invisible. As if I had some sort of plague. But I had my new Batman lunch box that I hoped would protect me from the endless cruelty. I stood stiff, ready to push myself up if I was knocked to the ground. Though soon I relaxed and watched a plump, white-and-gray pigeon land on the statue of Saint Francis, which was tucked in close to the red-brick school building. I had never really noticed him before.

Then Pam, a thin, light-black-skinned girl with wiry, unkempt hair ran up to me with a friendly smile. Was she coming to play with me or hit me? I had learned that a smile didn't mean someone was friendly. I was gullible and took everything at face value. The idea had come to me from animals; however, people were another story. Animals always communicated their intentions.

Pam ran up to me with startling eyes, murmuring so low that I had to strain to hear her, as I had chronic ear infections and was hard of hearing. I had failed the hearing test and second grade that year, then was moved from the back of the classroom, where I liked it, to the front, where I hated it, since I would often get called on.

Pam leaned in, and I could feel her breath on my cheek. In a soft whisper she said, "I would play with you, but then I'd get beat up too."

I said, "That's okay. Thanks." And smiled as if I had won the-almost-had-a-friend lottery.

Then I felt a flash of joy and sadness. I was sympathetic to her predicament. She ran off as quickly as she rushed in, and I was grateful for her not lingering since she might pay a price for even talking to me. I didn't want my almost new friend to get hurt.

A glimmer of hope washed over me that maybe one day I could be a beautiful swan. It awakened an idea that maybe this was just like the situation in the book. I would come into my own. I could be a swan!

Then another thought came to me that I wasn't liked because I didn't look anything like the children around me and had nothing to do with me having a Batman lunch box, a depravity if you were a girl to be punished by being called a boy. Which would be fine. I was supposed to be a boy anyway—my mother had told me so. But being called a boy was said as if it was as an insult, and I was the only girl I knew who had a boy lunch box. But I loved that lunch box. My neighborhood was populated by minorities, and I was a minority among them. At the time, I thought that was all there was to it.

I walked over to talk to the nuns, as I often did.

Sister Regina, our teacher and religion instructor, was a hard woman. Pale skinned and puffy cheeked, she hardly smiled, and she was also a liar. I discerned this when I asked her what color her hair was under her habit. She said it was blue and looked up. "Like the sky."

I said, in the most respectful way I could, "No." Then smiled and looked up at the sky, then back at the sister clothed in black with a halo of white around her head. "Really, what color is it, Sister?"

She just smirked and moved away from me, and I wondered if she would mention this desertion at her confession.

I followed the pigeon to the statue of Saint Francis. The pigeon cooed, and another one fluttered by and sat on the ledge of the larger windowsill. I walked back to the sister.

"Sister Regina? Who's that?" I pointed to Saint Francis.

She turned her whole body to look as if her head couldn't move freely of the long black robe or there was a real man standing beside her.

"Saint Francis," she replied.

"Who is he? Why does he have a dove on him and have animals?"

"It's Saint Francis of Assisi. He was the Patron Saint of Animals. He was their protector. He talks to them." She smiled. "He was an Italian."

"My mom is Italian!" I said, wondering if we could be related. "I love animals too!"

Was the pigeon sending me a message? Was I to be the guardian and caretaker of the animals as Saint Francis was? I had planned on being a superhero.

That idea of being a superhero came to me not long before when I was five. It was as I was watching a Tarzan movie. It was a good day for me and for Tarzan, who was beating the bad guys who had guns and wanted to kill everything and take over the world. But Tarzan had a secret weapon: the African wildlife was there to help him.

I wanted to be friends with wild animals, and that day it seemed possible to have big, wild adventures that would take me to exotic places. Believing with my whole heart that I would go to Africa and find Tarzan and we would be great friends. He would teach me how to swing on a rope. I would have a monkey. I would be strong and fight injustice and protect and love all the animals around me. I would make Tarzan and Batman proud. Yes, suddenly Batman left the cave of my imagination and was in Africa with Tarzan and me. I panicked, Batman in Africa? I had to fix this. I ran to the Batmobile of my imagination.

Batman and Tarzan should never meet; it would not be good to have the Batmobile in Africa. It would just scare all the critters. No, no, no!

I like that Tarzan lived in a tree, and it didn't seem right to invite Batman to Africa, because Batman had a cave and Tarzan had a tree. Maybe I could still become a veterinarian and work in the city with Batman, then take long trips to live wild adventures in the wilderness. Yes, that was more like it. I needed to be practical.

These thoughts of what to do and how to fit wild animals and superheroes into my future flew around in my head.

But just as it clicked in, then that day in the courtyard gave me a wish that I would grow out of being an ugly duckling and that the statue of Saint Francis intrigued me. I would add him to my list of heroes, along with Batman, Tarzan, and Superman. Heroes that I wanted to emulate to do good, be strong, and protect helpless animals and children. The pigeon drew me in, saying, *Pay attention to this! You're not the only one who sees that these animals have feeling and worth. To be connected to them is to be connected to God and the earth and yourself.* Could I be a guardian or caretaker of the animals as Saint Francis was? I had up to that point wanted to be a superhero. But what kind?

I thought I should pray to St. Francis. He must have been a good man, a superhero for animals, and maybe he could help me help them.

Although Sister Regina did plant a seed of doubt about her hair, and I would often stare at her head hoping to get a glimpse of the truth, I still liked her. She would be my second-grade teacher again when I failed second grade the first time around but not before betraying my trust before that first year was over.

Back in class she had picked me one day to spell a word. The word was *let*, and I couldn't spell it. She wrote it on the blackboard, and I still couldn't say it right.

"Put your hands out," she said, holding the ruler.

She then hit my outstretched hands over and over as she asked me again how to spell the three-letter word. Each time I spelled it wrong she hit my hands and asked me to try again. I spelled it backward and wrote it backward, then added an *i* instead of a *t* on the blackboard. It was humiliating, making it harder to spell or even talk. The kids nicknamed me "Dummy," which in a way was better than some of the other names they called me. With tears and snot rolling down my face the palms of my hand were red hot, then they went numb. I held them out in obedience, knowing what was coming. I thought of the stained-glass window in the church that depicted the crucifixion. I thought of Jesus and Joan of Arc and the others who had suffered for humanity, and it kept me from sinking to the floor. Yet it couldn't stop my crying that day in the class, then in the girls' bathroom as I ran the cold water over my hands and splashed my face. My heart was broken again, this time by Sister Regina, and I would no longer stand and talk to her in the courtyard. Instead I found a place to hide in the archway of the rectory on the opposite side of the courtyard.

I had become good at hiding—at home in the closet or in the doghouse or the yard or under the porch or behind the door when someone came over. I also hid my feeling as best I could and would be still and as silent as possible.

Tucked away I took comfort in the small courtyard and the low, sweet coos of the pigeons. I knew that day that I didn't see things as others did. Just like I couldn't see the *let* that looked like *tel* or *lel*, and that's how I spelled it. Sister Regina saw it as mocking; I could see it in her angry eyes. My mother wouldn't be happy with me getting left back as I did in second grade. And as Sister Regina hit me that day and on one other occasion, I would repeatedly disappoint my mother. She would ask why I couldn't be as smart as my sister who got straight As. I had no answer for her and would just hang my head in disappointment. One thing I did learn was to memorize the up-and-down shapes of the word *let*, like a picture in my head, and I would never spell that word wrong again. Being around liars was something I expected, and finding a childhood friend was something I had hoped for, but it never happened. So, when Pam came to me with a smile and didn't hit or push me, I was surprised, but it was the nuns who took a sacred oath and their betrayal surprised and hurt the most. It had left me with a distrust of humans, and I felt a dislike for myself that I didn't realize I had until the pigeon cooed and sent me back to that time.

Those memories made me want to destroy my art, and when I crumpled up and threw out my drawing, I cried.

Chapter 5:

Release of a Kraken

Sucking up the air as if I had been under water, I woke up not knowing I was dreaming, still struggling, kicking and punching the air, fighting with a past terror.

"Jo, Jo, wake up! You were screaming in your sleep again," Howard said.

"I'm sorry," I said, trying to bring myself back to this world.

He got up to get ready for work but didn't ask what I had been dreaming about.

It was like Zeus was releasing the Kraken, and again nightmares hijacked my dreams of lions in Africa, triggered by some unconscious event.

The dream had been recurring since I was nine. In it, I'm standing in the hallway of my house in Brooklyn. I'm not sure why I'm there. It's late, and I know I should be in bed.

I listen hard, and though the house is dead quiet, I don't hear any street noise, cars, or the L trains. It feels unnatural. I search my mind but can't recall how I got there. Was I sleepwalking? Then I hear the front door open and the creak of the wooden floor. I see a young man, and my heart races. He's an older teenager who looks rough, like the gangs I've seen beating people up in the subway and streets. He's invaded our house. I worry as I stand frozen.

Had the door been left open, or did he break in?

The man heads toward the downstairs apartment, and I worry about my mother and father. When I see him, I tuck myself against the wall. He stops. Even though I'm quiet he sees me. Did he spot me, or does he sense me there? Either way he starts to run up the stairs after me. It's then that I see the blade of a knife as it shimmers in the faint light. Terrified, I rush into the apartment. I'm in the kitchen and trying to close the apartment door. But I'm shaking and fumble with the flimsy hook-and-eye lock. I look over at the large windows. They have no curtains or shades. Its pitch black outside, and I feel exposed in the glaring lights overhead.

Tears of fear roll down my face.

I lean on the door with my weight, but I'm too small to hold it closed. The young man dressed in black pushes open the door with a bang, and I fall back.

I'm face-to-face with him. I catch his wild and desperate eyes. He scans the room for what's worth stealing. I look at the case against the wall that holds our charming collections of china. A milk creamer, silver spoons from the world fair, and other heirlooms. The things I take out often. That fascinate me. Things I love to sit and touch in wonder of their history. Who bought them and why? What meaning did they hold to those people?

I mumble incoherent words. I'm shaking and know he means to hurt me if he doesn't get what he wants. But I don't know what he wants. I try to remain calm and look around for someplace to go. I move slowly and feel as if I'm floating around the kitchen table. I want to run back to my room. But I can't. He won't let me. I see the knife held tight in his fist, ready to strike. He grabs me by the hair and slams me to the floor. I scream, but no one comes. My screams are hollow and empty. He sits on top of me, suffocating me. I become mute. I want to make a sound but can't.

He starts stabbing me in the chest, over and over. At first, I feel nothing. Then there's a burring pain in my chest. I can't breathe, and then I disappear. An emptiness washes over me. I reappear as nothing but a thought. A ghost without a body floating above the scene, emotionless to what I can see happening to me. The room goes dark and light again, and I see myself in a coffin in the same kitchen. I see my mother, father, and sister talking and moving around me as I lay lifeless, hands folded in front of me, dead. It was as if I wasn't there and never existed. I want to say, *I'm here! I'm here!* But nothing comes out.

Even though I'm an adult now, I'm always a nine-year-old in my dreams. They were always the same with only smaller details changed. Sometimes two men would break in to the house instead of one or the door to the front of the house would be wide open and he'd walk in. Sometimes the bad men wore bandanas—red, blue, or any of the colors of different gangs. One thing that never changed was that I would always be at the top of the stairs and die in the dream.

It was strange that Howard never asked about the dreams or said much about the photo. The self-portrait where I was sure he would see my discontent, my isolation.

There was something missing in me and us. I made a list of all the good things in my head. He spelled words for me. He seemed confident—something I longed to be. We both loved music. He was funny and liked animals too.

When I was late for my orientation and my first day of college, he helped me as I cried in a phone booth on the side of the road.

"What's wrong?" He'd sounded annoyed, and I'd felt guilty for calling him at work.

"I can't go to college."

"What's wrong with you? You just went through all this, and now you're not going to go?"

"But I'm late! I'm always late! I'm missing orientation. I can't go!"

"I have to get back to work. Just go. It's okay; you just missed orientation."

"Really? You really think I should go?"

"Yes! I'll see you later."

He loves me, I thought as I hung up the phone. I considered how he had to put up with me as I got back in the car and thought about how lucky I was to have him.

Yet, when I wanted to put the school bumper sticker on our hot rod of a car, he said no.

"Why? It's my car too," I pleaded. "I'll put it in the back window, not on the bumper."

"No, I don't want it on the car."

We yelled at each other all the way to me dropping him off at his job. I sped away as he thew the cup of coffee he had just bought at the car.

We fought that night because he'd said everyone saw it and that he was humiliated.

I set up to paint that Sunday and worked on a painting of horses in a field under the moonlight. Mellissa was at her cousin's house for the day, and it took me forever to set up my oil paints since there was no room for me to have a real studio. Still, it was better than our last apartment where I only had a small kitchen table in a dark space.

Cleaning up took almost as much time as it did for me to paint.

Howard came home from the store just as I was starting to work. He had a sack of beer and chips.

"I thought you were going to watch the game," I said.

"They're coming over here," he said.

"But I just started painting."

"You going to make something?"

"I'm painting."

"They'll be here in a minute."

Was he requesting or demanding?

"Okay, I'll be quiet," was my solution.

"But who's going to cook?" he asked.

"I don't know, I'm painting. I just set up, and it takes me a long time to do this and clean up after. The light is good now."

The only place to paint was in the front room of the bungalow I was sharing with a fancy-tailed white pigeon that I'd found with a hurt wing and was nursing him back to health. The room had a lot of windows, and the pigeon liked looking outside. He also watched me paint with our rescue dog, Billy, who looked more like a black wolf and was under my feet, sound asleep.

It was my own fault that he wanted me to cook and serve his friends. I had done it so many times before. I loved that everyone loved my cooking. It was the one thing I was sure I was good at and fed on the desires and requests for some of the dishes I made. I learned how to cook mostly from my father and grandmother.

It made me feel good to feed others and see them happy, fussing over everyone to make my husband proud to have me as his wife.

Look pretty, smile, and be the spitting image of a '50s TV-show housewife.

But that was changing, and I wanted to paint more than I wanted to serve his friends.

"Order a pizza," I said looking at my canvas.

I could see by his furrowed eyebrows that he was pissed. Soon his friends were at the door. Thinking that would be the end of it, I kept painting but felt the hole burring though me as my husband seemed more obsessed with me feeding and getting drinks for his friends than the game. He came in and out of the room more times than I could count. It was getting harder to concentrate, and I felt like destroying the painting altogether. I thought this would make us both happy to do what we wanted. But it didn't.

His friends left early, sensing the tension, then we had a fight.

When I finished the painting of the horses under the moonlight, I gave it away. I didn't even take a photo of it. My mind was spinning with confused emotions, and I had a lot to think about.

But like Scarlett O'Hara in *Gone with the Wind* I would put off thinking about it in a tomorrow that never seemed to come. Until it did.

CHAPTER 6:
THE SPAGHETTI-BABY LUNCHEON

I t was at the end of my second year of school after that self-portrait photo that my hair started to fall out. It was difficult to keep up carrying eighteen credits and working weekends—my body and husband told me so. By my third year the pressure became too much and I caved.

With a lack of funds for school supplies and barely being able to make ends meet at home, attending school full time was no longer an option.

Now I was working full time and taking classes at night, and I was heartbroken over it. To me, it was just another failure. There wasn't a day on my long train rides from the city and back to work that I didn't think I might ever reach my goal of having a bachelor's degree in art. The thought of quitting frightened me so much that I couldn't give it up altogether. Even though it felt like I was. So, I settled for going part time with school three nights a week after work at the advertising company where I was doing typesetting for car ads.

The idea I had of pushing myself to go to college and giving my daughter a better future became hazy. All I could see now were my shortcomings about not being a better wife and mother.

And it wasn't just that. I couldn't help but believe that I was guilty in my purpose of giving my daughter a better life and a well-educated mother and that somehow she would resent me for not being home every night to cook her dinner and help with her homework.

I did cook homemade meals in the mornings before work. And on Sundays I made homemade marinara with fresh tomatoes, if I had them, as well as soups. Then I would freeze them for the upcoming week. But I wasn't there to eat them with her three nights a week.

It was fine, I told myself. It would get easier soon, we would spend more time together.

It was okay not to have all the art supplies I needed. Even though it pained me at times, like when I missed out on what Melissa did that day or when I needed something like photo paper or to paint over canvases I wanted to keep. Also, it was when my professor had asked to see all my paintings from his class.

"Why?" I'd asked.

"We're having a group show, and I want to include one of your paintings," he'd said.

But there were only two to choose from.

"Where's the rest of them?" he'd inquired, looking confused.

My palms were sweaty, and my words came out sounding broken. "This is all of them. I had to paint over them."

"Why did you do that?"

"I can't afford it. I have a daughter, and I have to work. The school loan didn't cover everything. I'm sorry."

"That's a shame," he said

By destroying my paintings, by painting over them, I realized I couldn't see my progress.

Progress. Did I really have any, or was I just winging it? Was I just painting over some of my dreams?

Torn between my career and domestic life, I felt myself caving.

One of my night classes was an advanced airbrushing class. I had taught myself how to airbrush and incorporated it into some of my work. I wanted to learn more. I also wanted to find out more about what disturbed me in the eyes of my photo. My class project would be a painting of that self-portrait. But I never finished it. I didn't want to look at it anymore, so I put it away. I was already feeling like I was at a crossroads for change but didn't know what kind of changes I should make.

Then the Friday before Mother's Day my five-year-old daughter triggered some real changes in all our lives.

Yet they weren't the internal changes I should have or was hoping to make before I brought another life into this world.

Melissa's school was having a Mother's Day spaghetti luncheon.

The school staff were wonderful, and she was happy there. It gave me peace of mind that she was safe and well taken care of while I was in school or working.

It was her last year there, as she would be graduating to public school.

When I entered the classroom, Melissa was standing by the small round table in her classroom. The table had a white paper tablecloth and paper plates, forks, and a paper cup for every little wooden chair. She was wearing gray pants, as she didn't like to wear dresses. She had on a white, gray, and pink-striped long-sleeve shirt with Keds sneakers and hot-pink bow clips in her hair.

"Mommy!" she shouted. She was so excited. She ran to me, took my hand, and rushed me to the table. I sunk down into the small chair. She climbed on my lap and gave me a hug, then handed me my cards and a gift of a plant that Melissa said she had picked out herself. She gave me a purple African violet and a card made out of craft paper that I saved, as I did all her gifts and cards. Then we ate cold spaghetti. Shortly after everyone got up to clean and leave for the day she climbed back on my lap and dropped a baby bomb.

"Mommy, I want a baby sister."

"Oh, honey," I said and hugged her.

"Can we have a baby?" she pleaded.

"Do you really want a sister? What if it was a boy?"

She thought about it for a moment and said yes.

Had I deprived my daughter of a sibling? Was she lonely? These questions tore at me. It was always my dream to have more children, and I even considered adopting a child in need. I told Howard what Melissa had said. After that, Howard and I talked quite a bit about it. "We should try for another baby," I said, and he agreed.

A year later, I got pregnant.

When I left my job at the advertising company, the staff threw me a surprise party with gifts and a white painter's hat signed by everyone in the office with little paintings and drawings next to their names to remember them by. Touched by the gift, I hung it on the corner of my drafting table at home. When I left that day, I was sad to say goodbye, but I was also saying hello to a new way of life. Still, I wanted that little piece of paper to prove to myself that I wasn't stupid or a quitter. I wasn't ready to give up that dream just yet.

So, with a big belly I waddled into classes two nights a week in hopes I could still get my bachelor's degree. But it was time for me to focus more on my family and push my career aside—for now, anyway. The self-portrait slumbered in a drawer—I was still not ready to see the truth in my own eyes.

CHAPTER 7:
TOMATO GOODBYES

I had stayed in school until the end of the semester and had hopes of going back to finish my last year. During my pregnancy I was able to get a job working part time at home making Mardi Gras masks with the woman who ran a home-based business a few blocks away.

But I had left the new job at seven months pregnant as I was too swollen to do anything. The doctor insisted on bed rest, as it was a hard pregnancy, and I was sick most of the time.

I gave birth in the fall two weeks after my birthday.

Howard had spent most of my pregnancy at work, the gym, or out with friends. He was in great shape, but our baby, who we named Julianne, didn't know his voice or face, so she cried when he held her, like he was a stranger. Two months after the baby was born Melissa, who had asked for a baby sister, was now asking if we could send the baby back.

"No, honey. She'll grow out of this," I said referring to the colic and constant crying. She looked at me with doubt.

Julianne was so different from Melissa as a baby, who was so easy and quiet, sleeping through the night from the start. As I had helped raising my little sister and brother, I had experience with babies but had never seen a baby sleep all night in the first few months. Standing over Julianne's crib I would often pray she would sleep more than an hour or two. I didn't sleep for the first six months. She was colic and hated the car and would scream the whole way to and from wherever we went.

So, it made going back to work difficult.

By the next summer Julianne grew out of her colic stage and was sleeping, crawling, and in a walker.

"Missy," I said, "my little helper. I want you to help Mommy baby-proof the house. It's fun. I did it when you started crawling around." Melissa was in on the game, and we got down on all fours like Billy, who ran over to play, waging his curled-up, fluffy tail.

I said, "Okay, we have to pretend we're a baby and crawl around and look for anything babies can't have and give it to Mommy. Then what do you say we go to the store and make something yummy?" She giggled through the whole thing.

When we had rented the beach bungalow, even though the front yard was mostly concrete, it had a small patch of sandy dirt by the cyclone fence that separated the tiny yards. I had planned on growing tomatoes in hopes of passing on a love of nature and gardening to my daughter. But I was having a hard time in the sandy soil.

Wanting to make fried green tomatoes and not having any in my pathetic garden, I drove down to the fish market to buy some. The owner's wife had a garden in the back of the lot and sold fresh produce and green tomatoes.

It was too hot, and I was too sick the summer I was pregnant. Busy being a mom of two there was no time to paint either. So my creativity turned to the kitchen with slanted floors and cabinets and appliances from the Dark Ages where I was starting to teach Melissa about cooking. We made sauce and homemade bread and apple pie.

My kitchen wasn't the dream kitchen I had always desired, but I had no complaints, as it was a step up from a boarding room I rented at seventeen and the one-car-garage apartment I had shared with Howard when we first lived together. It had a hot plate and toaster oven and a fridge, and I had learned at an early age to be resourceful. I cooked full dinners from scratch for my husband and his friends. Now I was making homemade baby food after discovering my baby had allergies, which helped with her tummy woes.

My father would stop by the house regularly now that I was home. He would take Melissa for a walk to the ice cream stand five blocks away. Then on the way back he would give her a dollar to buy some candy. Sitting on the stoop rocking the baby I watched as they walked back, and it almost made me cry to see them holding hands like two children trying to catch the drips of vanilla running down the cone before it reached their fingers. That was something I had wished he would have done with me when I was Melissa's age.

My father had gotten work sometimes as a handyman, and when I was in my early twenties, I sometimes went on jobs with him. He was well-liked by everyone who hired him and got most jobs by word of mouth. But he was unreliable. I painted a railing while he tarred a roof on a hot summer day. Before we started, we stopped at a deli he liked and brought me out a big hero of sausages, peppers, and too many onions. It was too early in the morning for such a big onion-filled meal. But I ate it because he got it for me, and it was one of the first times I felt like his daughter and we shared a moment. It was before I started college and after I'd had Melissa. He said he needed the help with the job, and I needed the money. We had spent the whole day togeth-er, and for that whole day I felt what I saw as Melissa and my father walked down the street together. It was what made me choke up and also feel resentful at the same time.

Melissa loved him so much, and this allowed me to see him in a different light. He wasn't the same man I grew up with, and I wanted to forget the meanness and had to push away the memories.

Like in the shows or movies I watched as a child I had believed people were either good or bad, not in between. It was a lie. It confused me how someone could be kind and unkind, sometimes in the same day. Now I had at least progressed from that black-and-white thinking. Watching my father and daughter walk down the street I saw proof that things can change. Even though it was hard and I felt like I missed out on that father. Even so, it made me happy to see past my own bias of who my father had been to me and who he was now.

He was the first man I loved and in my young eyes should have been perfect. Yet he had strayed so far from the man I was seeing now. My daughter was helping me remember the bits and pieces of the love that the ill-treatment and neglect and drama had taken away.

Melissa ran to me so excited. "Look what Grandpa gave me," she said, holding up a dollar.

"It's for later," he said, sitting down in the living room as he pol-ished off the last bit of the cone, asking if I needed anything fixed.

I wondered if he realized I didn't let her eat a lot of sweets.

"Well," I said, "the kitchen faucet is leaking. Howard tried to fix it, but it still leaks."

My father got up and went to get his tools from the old, rusted, hand-painted van in front of the house. He was very handy, and although I never saw him have a real job, he did odds and ends. I had imagined that his father had taught him, but I didn't know. He taught me how to fix just about anything. I could have fixed the sink myself or called the landlord, but I didn't. I liked that he wanted to help.

Wiping his hands after he had fixed the leak he began explaining why Howard couldn't get the job done. "He's just a young buck." My father gestured to the fixed faucet. "He tried to tighten it too much. You know that's why women make good plumbers—they have a gentle touch. Yeah." he continued staring off to somewhere in the past. "I was just like Howard at his age, all filled with fire, angry at the world. Using brute force like a gorilla."

Then he laughed. I didn't.

I listened and hung on every word my father said, as if I was trying to decipher some hidden code in them. I asked him if he wanted a cup of coffee.

Julianne was in her walker and made a beeline to him, jumping, drooling, and cooing.

A smile spread across his face as he patted her head. "She's a pip, that one."

Father's Day came around, and I stopped by to see my father in the morning since I was going to spend the rest of the day with my husband and the girls. I was out shopping for groceries to make my husband a special dinner. I had already gotten him some presents but was in the drugstore picking out a card and frantic as to what to get my father since I felt that the wallet I got him wasn't enough. I saw the carrousel of sunglasses. He had never had a pair.

So, I tried a bunch on, then chose a pair I thought would look good on him. I picked out a funny card as a sentimental one for him felt unnatural. I stopped to get him some other small things, put it all in a gift bag, and drove over to the apartment.

It was the same small two-bedroom basement apartment that we had moved to when I was fifteen. It was after the fire where I lost everything, and now almost fourteen years later they were still there. The one my mother said we would only live in for a few months, as there were three children sharing one small room—and for a while one bed.

When I pulled up my father was sitting on the side of the house smoking and drinking a beer.

"Hey," I said holding the gift bag. "What's going on?" I sat at the worn-out picnic table. There was a big root of a plant on the table. "What's that?"

He squinted and looked tired. "It's a horseradish root I've been growing." He nodded gesturing to the weed-filled patch next to the fence.

"Really? I've never seen one before. I'm going to try and grow tomatoes, but the soil is so sandy, and I only have that small patch. I didn't think you could grow anything because the plot is so small. It's hard with all the sand."

I got up to examine the small patch of earth next to the fence.

"Happy Father's Day," I said. turning back to him, I picked up the bag and held it out.

"Ow, look at that," he said, looking at the bag then taking a drag off his cigarette.

"Where's Mom?" I asked looking up at the closed door. *They must be fighting*, I thought. It was too hot to keep the door closed. Then I felt bad for him sitting here alone on Father's Day.

He sighed. "She's inside."

"Oh." I put the bag down and pushed it closer to him. "Why don't you open it?"

"I can do it later." He took a sip of beer. He was always shy and awkward about getting presents. But I wanted him to see the sunglasses. He squinted in the sun, and I wanted him to be more comfortable. I reached in the bag and took out the sunglasses and fake-leather wallet.

"See?" I said, eager. I handed him the sunglasses. "I got you sunglasses and a new wallet. Try them on."

He fumbled for a moment with the items, then put them on. They were black Ray-Bans, and once they were on I could no longer see his bloodshot eyes.

"Oh, these are great," he said. He looked over the wallet like there was some mystery about what it was.

"I had seen you needed a new wallet and never had sunglasses before. They look good."

"Thanks," he said and seemed to drift away.

I hated seeing him like that. He had gone so long this time. I opened the door to check on my mother. She was watching TV. She had gotten work cleaning houses, and I was teaching her how to drive so she could get her license. I was happy that she was doing things for herself.

I asked how she was, and she told me about work.

"That's great. I'll see you later. Gotta go for now."

I slipped out the door. I swallowed hard and felt a lump in my throat. It was hot, and I began to sweat and wanted to go.

"Howard got the kids, and I got to go shopping. Happy Father's Day!"

I walked away, then looked back to see his head hung low and wondered if he had been up all night.

The next day I drove over to check on him.

I knocked on the screen of the open door and called in, "Mom?" She came out to the living room. "Hey. I stopped by to see how he was. Where is he?"

"He's sleeping," she said. "Look what your father gave me." Then she put on the sunglasses. It was the pair I had given him the day before. Then with the sunglasses still on she showed me the wallet and said, "This too."

"Wow, that's really nice. They look good on you."

"Yeah, we had a fight, and then he gave me this. They look good, right?"

"Yes," I said. I wanted to weep. Did he not like them? "Okay, I gotta go. Say hi for me."

Then I went home and tried to focus on my family, but my thoughts kept wandering to the apartment and if my father was okay. He had been doing so well for a while.

As I cooked, I distracted myself with other thoughts. I realized I would have to find a way to make more money. Howard never made enough, and even if he did, he would go through his pay like a glass of water in the desert. I would sell my artwork, but it wasn't enough. I also wanted to be home with the kids more. How was I going to do that and take care of kids full time? Finishing school would have to wait.

That Christmas I was going to give as many handmade presents as possible in order to save money. Melissa got a purple Mardi Gras mask, her favorite color, and I made hand-painted clothing with animals—a tiger, zebras, and some with abstract shapes for my girls and their cousins. When Melissa opened all her presents, she cried when she opened the Mardi Gras mask.

"What's wrong?" I asked.

"I wanted one for so long. And you made one for me," she said

"Oh, sweetie, I didn't know it meant that much to you." I hugged and kissed her. "Let's hang it up in your room."

It was a good Christmas, and it made me delight in the idea that personal gifts meant more to my daughter than store-bought ones.

A week after Christmas I went to visit Howard's cousin in Queens. We had become friends, and she had two little ones too. Her husband had his own business, and they were doing well.

The kids settled in to play, and she poured the tea.

"You know, Jo," she said as she sat down, "I love the hand-painted clothes you made and would like to order a few for gifts."

"That's okay, Randy, I can make them for you, just pay for the shirts. Everyone seems to like them, and I've been getting some orders."

I looked down at my tea feeling embarrassed.

"Jo, I'm telling you, you can sell these. I shop at the boutiques. I know."

I felt myself turning red.

"I don't know how."

"Get a pad and put some samples together and go up and down the boulevard." She was referring to the wealthy part of Long Island.

A month or so later I did as she said and walked in the first fancy boutique. I had never been in one before and felt like a caveman in a china shop trying to blend in.

No was the answer. "We're not buying right now." I almost packed up and walked out, but then I had a flash of my life working back in the city and missing out on seeing my kids come home from school.

"That's okay," I said smiling and pulling out my dollar-store receipt pad. "How about I just leave some with you? If you sell them, great! If not, I'll be back next week around the same time to pick them up. No obligation. Nothing to lose."

Without waiting for a response, I wrote on the pad what I was leaving, how much the wholesale price was, and my phone number. I said the same thing for every boutique I went into after that, adding that so and so's boutique has them in there store right now. "But not the same designs, of course."

It worked, and I went home with an empty bag and two messages on my phone.

They both said the same thing: "JoAnne, we sold out on the clothes and would like you to bring more."

I played the messages a few more times, then picked up the baby and Melissa and danced around the room with them and told Howard when he got home.

"That's great," he said. "You're goanna make some money from all this?"

"Yes" was my response, but I really wasn't sure. I just wanted to try. It always felt like Howard was being callous when I came home with news of any accomplishments. It was a disturbing but familiar place to be. At home in Brooklyn, it often felt like every day was a put-down. But now it had become my fuel to prove my husband wrong about me.

By spring I had ten boutiques buying from me and had to hire help. When the boutique only a mile from my house put my stuff in the window, I drove by with the girls.

"See? Those are Mommy's clothes."

I was proud of myself for the first time in a long time.

Maybe I can start taking a class or two soon, I thought. *As soon as the baby gets a little older.*

I was also determined to plant some tomatoes in that patch of sand. It was a nice spring day and warm enough. The girls played in the front yard while I pulled the weeds and poured the bag of soil, then planted the tomatoes I grew from seeds I had saved. Melissa had dressed Billy in Julianne's bonnet. Billy was a patient dog but was looking for me to save him. I laughed and said, "I'm sorry, Billy," and took a picture of him in the bonnet.

Standing up, hose in hand, I felt satisfied and confident about growing my tomatoes and was looking forward to a bright future. I was already craving fried green tomatoes.

Making fried green tomatoes was a summer tradition I shared with my father on his good days. He had taught me how to geminate the seeds, grow the plants, pick the green ones, take the bitterness out, and how to fry them. Every summer the memory and his voice flooded my mind each time I picked up a homegrown tomato. The first time we grew tomatoes together I was five. It wasn't long after planting the tomatoes that spring that I got the phone call I was dreading that I knew one day would come. It was my mother.

"Your father's in the hospital, and they're going to admit him. He was throwing up blood." She was crying. "He's in the ICU."

"I'll head down now."

The antiseptic smell in the hospital made me feel sick. But I straightened up before I entered my father's room in the ICU. I pulled up a chair, and as I sat across from him, I watched his hands shake while eating ice chips in the bed. He looked down and around but not at me, and as frightened as I felt inside I still gave him a weak smile and sat up straight, as I was beginning to slouch, in a compliance of what I was often told as a girl. I kept my cool just like I did the day I got lost in Central Park on a school trip and had to beg for change to take the subway home. He often talked about how I was swinging my pocketbook with my sunglasses on without a care in the world. But that was my way of hiding my fear as I did now in the ICU waiting and watching my father slowly disappear. I couldn't save him. But I wanted to help distract him from what he was going through. So I came back and brought the *Reader's Digest* and *Consumer Report.* He was once well-off as a child, but after my grandfather died, my father blew through the money, and by the time I was five we were very poor. After that he never bought anything new, and now he never would. No new TV, car, or appliances. But he liked knowing what the best-quality product was. I read to him for a while, hoping he would find comfort in the distractions.

I told him what *Consumer Report* said was the best car or refrigerator or radio on the market and why. I had nothing else to say about appliances and vehicles and what they were showing on TV that week.

Soon came the awkward silences.

I didn't like them, and I didn't know what to say. I stayed every day as long as I could watching my mother and siblings and a few friends come and go.

I grasped at straws of thought. In my mind I was walking through the house looking for my baby, worrying that she thought I had abandoned her because I was spending so much time at the hospital. How could I tell my Melissa that the grandfather she adored was dying? Then I thought about my sad garden at the bungalow in the tiniest patch of sandy dirt.

I cleared my throat and said with a renewed but strained voice, "The tomatoes are dying, and I don't know what to do."

I corrected my choice of words and said I was having some trouble with the garden.

We had a long history of talking about and planting tomatoes. It had started when I was young. I had found a bunch of small terracotta pots in the back of the junkyard and asked what they were for, then if we could plant something. My father made a sandwich. He was a great cook and could make the most amazing meals from whatever we had in the kitchen. Which was either a short feast or a long famine. But when he made the sandwich, he cut into the juicy, red, ripe tomato, and the seeds fell out. He scoped them up and placed them on a paper towel. He taught me how to make fried green tomatoes. To pluck them just before they turn and soak them in salt and sugar to cut the bitterness. It was our way of connecting.

I felt numb, and my children wanted me home. But I couldn't leave my father alone. So we talked about tomatoes because we couldn't talk about anything else. We couldn't talk about the fact that he was dying. We couldn't talk about how much we loved each other—or didn't. I would never really know now if he truly loved me, but he must have. There would be no hugs or kisses or dramatic goodbyes. We didn't talk about or say anything important. He never told me he loved me, nor did I expect it.

Instead I told him that the trouble was planting the tomatoes by the beach, that the dirt was mostly sand. I said this as I held back tears. He looked away.

I said I didn't think they were going to make it this year. That the new baby, work, cooking, cleaning, and doing homework with Melissa had left me little time for the garden. He looked down and stirred his ice chips with shaky hands. He gave me a few tips, like always. He asked if it got enough sun. I couldn't remember.

I said they wilted and were so small and looked like they were dying. He told me not to worry about it. He said that they would come back.

I stepped out for some air and cried in my car.

When I came back my father was reaching out his hand to me, and I went to take it before the nurse pulled me away as the alarms went off on the monitoring machines.

Pushed in to the hallway of the ICU I looked at my father's pleading eyes, wanting to go to him. The doctor came to me with a sheet of paper and a pen to sign a release to put my father on a ventilator. I hesitated. It didn't feel right, and I had questions. But the doctor pressured me. "You want him to be more comfortable, don't you?" He stood in the doorway in between my father and me and kept pushing for me to sign, repeating, "You want him to be more comfortable? This will make him more comfortable"

"Yes, yes," I said shaking and tearing up. "But can I ask him?" I looked over at my father who appeared terrified.

"There's no time," the doctor said.

I reluctantly signed the paper, and they made me leave. All I could see as I waited was my father's outstretched hand, that no one would let me hold, and the terror in his eyes. I knew that moment would replay in my mind and haunt me forever. Signing those papers would be a decision I hated myself for once I saw the results. His eyes bulged out of his head, and he could no longer speak. He would have no last words. He didn't look more comfortable; he looked terrified with the tube breathing for him. I took his hand, and he weakly squeezed it as tears flowed down my face. Then I ran to the bathroom and threw up. I sat and cried on the cold tiled floor. I wanted to scream, to break something. I ran the cold water on my face and took deep breaths, then brushed my hair and went back to the room. I felt weak. I was at a loss about what to do, so I just talked. I told him he could let go, that he could go home now anytime he wanted.

He had been asking to go home all week, and I wanted to help him. Even if it could no longer be in his body.

Around two in the morning, I returned home exhausted. Howard awoke. I sobbed as I sat on the edge of the bed.

"Howard, I came out of the hospital and forgot where I parked. I couldn't find the car."

Howard never lifted his head off the pillow, but I could hear the anger in his voice. "Why do you stay there so long? Come home, the kids need you!"

"But this is the end. How could I just leave him alone?"

I don't remember what he said as I fell away into my own thoughts of guilt. Guilt for signing the papers, for not telling him how I really felt, for not being home for my family.

The day he died I woke up in a panic and called my friend to watch the girls. I sped down the road. Somehow, I knew that was the day. I needed to be there, but as I drove there was a helicopter in the sky. I had never seen one there before, and I bent forward to look at it. Suddenly everything felt as if it was in slow motion. The song "Don't Let the Sun Go Down on Me" by Elton John came on the radio, and

I knew he had passed. I looked up to the sky and knew I was too late and that my worst fear had come true—that he would die alone in the hospital.

When I got to the hospital, I was prepared for the news and asked to see him. He had passed not ten minutes before. He left his body at the same time as the song had come on and the helicopter had passed overhead. A thought entered my mind as I stared at my father's pale, motionless body: *Oh, that's not him anymore. The soul does leave the body.*

He had died alone.

I went to the bathroom and thew up again.

At the funeral I was shaking, then my father's voice was in my head, along with the memory of our last conversation, which would replay every time I picked a tomato from my garden. "You see this?" I could hear his voice as clear as day. I fell into a trance and was teleported to a time when I was five.

My father was standing in the sun pointing at the striped roly-poly as it made its way up the stem of a tomato plant.

"This little guy would eat the whole plant if you let him."

I didn't realize this day would become one of my strongest and best memories of my father or that tomatoes would be one of the last things I'd ever talk with him about.

He would pluck the caterpillar off the leaf, over and over again in my mind. Around us, a half dozen tomato plants grew in the small sunny spot behind the shed that I helped plant.

I leaned closer.

"What is it?" I asked.

"It's a caterpillar now, but it will be a butterfly one day."

When we had lived in Brooklyn, I'd only seen butterflies on rare occasions and believed them to be magic wing spirits, colorful and delicate, and I loved them for their fragile beauty. It was incredible how they endured so many transformations. From a pin-sized egg to a caterpillar, then as small angels that ventured out into the world with paper wings. As the caterpillar crawled on me it tickled my hand, and as my dad spoke, I saw a childlike wonder and sparkle in his eyes. It made me happy to see him pleased, even if only for a moment. It was the way I coped with the two sides of my father. It smoothed out the terrible traumas of a childhood living with an alcoholic. When he was his true self, he was kind but strict. Proud of his German heritage, a skilled cook who loved to garden.

It was a whole year later in that same small patch in the front yard of the same bungalow against the chain-link fence that I broke down and cried over the tomatoes that wouldn't grow there in the sand. I hated them for not growing.

But I was really crying over the loss of my father and all the things I never got to say or hear from him. The words I wanted to say but didn't because there was no more time.

I love you.

It was too hard for me to garden anymore, so I got up and walked away and let my tomatoes die.

CHAPTER 8:

REHAB 101

Five years had passed since my father died, about three since we moved from the beach, and a few thirty-somethings birthdays that slipped away faster than a second-hand clock moves.

It was Sunday morning, and I was preparing a feast of a breakfast, as I usually did for my family on Sundays, to be followed by another Sunday feast for dinner.

Breakfast was pancakes from scratch, fresh-squeezed orange juice, eggs, and about five other things. After breakfast the girls headed out for play dates and teen wanderings. Howard left to see his friend's new car. It was a blue Corvette convertible; a car Howard was pining for. We were married for over a dozen years now, and it was becoming more and more clear that we had very little in common besides the girls.

After cleaning up, I sat down with a hot cup of tea to read the *New York Times*, which had become my window to a world I wanted to live in, where artists lived their true life and scientists and naturalists explored, where I found the reminders of others living their dreams. I wanted to be one of them, featured in the paper, living my dream life, but it was still so far away. I had touched it once and believed that I could touch it again. Once over lunch I had confessed my desires to a friend. "It would be nice to be written up in the *Times* one day, like those artists I read about every Sunday."

She scoffed at me. "Jo, I wouldn't get my hopes up for that one."

I remained silent, as always, and looked away. It hurt, and I thought about it after. I had expected Howard to say something like that but not my friend. If I were to ever make it, I would have to believe in myself and not look for support from others—even my own friends.

While I sat in the living room of the house we bought that I didn't love, I scanned the newspaper for something, anything to help get me through another mind-numbing day.

Our new house was a thirty-minute drive to the beach and boardwalk that used to be only a block away. I was missing my walks beside the ocean that fed my soul. The sound of the seagulls and the woosh of the waves. The damp, salty air. The memories of being a teenager and a place that never betrayed or hurt me. Howard wanted the house because it was close to his new business but far from the ocean.

Still, it was a step up from the small bungalow we had rented with slanted floors, and I was determined to make the best of it.

The beach had been an anchor for me since our move to Long Island when I was a teenager. A year or two before I left the ghetto for good, I had become depressed, and by fourteen I'd stopped eating enough to sustain me and became alarmingly thin. I didn't know that I was depressed. No one I knew then used that word. I just wasn't hungry anymore and didn't want to talk to anyone. I would sit by the window in our upstairs apartment looking out and feeling nothing. No one was coming to save me. My family seemed like strangers. Any conversation back then was task or performance driven. *Did you do the dishes? Did you do your homework? Did you? Did you? Did you?* was all I heard.

No one wanted to know how I felt about anything. After a long while my mother took me to the doctor. I don't know if it was because the school called or because I became so noticeably thin. The doctor examined me and asked why I wasn't eating.

"I'm not hungry," I said.

Back then we were taught to be seen, not heard. Kids had no right to question anything, so it spilled over to how I communicated.

When I graduated from sixth grade, my school closed its doors for good. It could no longer stay open in such a poor, violent neighborhood. I volunteered to help every day after school for a while. I had started volunteering my time when I was in third grade to help the first-graders read, then by fifth grade I would help clean the church and oil the benches. Then I swept the floor and dusted the shelves and desks and packed the books.

I never wanted to go home and hung around the church schoolyard after I was done. Some kids from the neighborhood always played handball or basketball. Sometimes I would get to play handball. But most times I would wait until everyone left in hopes of shooting a few hoops. But the older boys were there. They would often come after school was out and take over. Then one day, as I sat on the stone wall watching, a fight broke out, as they often did. I heard shouting and became alarmed. This one felt different. Then one of the guys left yelling and waving his arms that he was going to come back and shoot the other one. I weighed out the odds of this happening and decided I should go. It was then two of the kids that left came back, and one had a gun and shot the other one. I'd thought they were friends, or maybe they were just gang members and not friends at all. Or they fought over the court. I never really knew. I don't remember if I saw the actual shooting as I blocked it out. It just seemed like one of my dreams. Yet I couldn't get over the fact that he had died over a basketball game. I couldn't wrap my head around the *why* of it. It made me want to shout, *It was just a game!* I felt my stomach turn. But I showed nothing but control and calmness when I got home that day.

My mother had given me permission to stay after school but not to hang around the schoolyard. I was there, and I was a witness. Everybody saw me there and knew we lived around the corner from the school and church. Rats and snitches often died where I lived.

If I was in shock, I didn't know it because I had already seen so much violence. I don't remember what I said to my mom or if I told her any of the details since everything was becoming a blur, like my memory of the event had fallen into quicksand. I was losing myself. The police asked me questions, and I told them all I knew about what had happened. After I sat in my room that night looking at the rosary that hung on the post of my bed, I curled up in a ball humming and rocking myself to sleep as I had done so many nights before.

After graduation I was told to pack some clothes.

"Why?" I'd asked my mother.

"You're going to stay with Clair by the beach."

I didn't ask any more questions. There was no reason to. To me, it was all just so sad. A sad place, with sad, angry people who had lost all hope, and I had embraced that club. The lost, the hopeless, the forsaken.

I got a garbage bag and put some clothes inside but wasn't allowed to take anything else. Not my dog, not my journals—nothing but an empty soul.

Staying with my godmother, a woman I hardly knew, the long walks on the beach were cathartic. The sand and peaceful ocean calmed me. The ocean had spoken to me, and I had cried at its shores. I listened to it like a newborn hearing its mother speak in a language I was just beginning to understand. The beach became my pacifier, my therapist, my friend.

Now I was searching in a newspaper for something to fill the void. To wake me up, but I didn't know what it could be till I was several pages into the *Times'* nature section. I was thinking of the beach and the dull day ahead when I felt excitement that I hadn't had for a long time. Like a jolt of adrenaline, it filled my head and body with energy. There was an article that said they needed volunteers to help with the wildlife center, and it was within half an hour of my house. So, the next day I called them to offer my time, though I had none to spare. But I knew I'd never have the time if I didn't make it. That time would be sucked up by chores and endless to-do lists, then my life would end. It was my life, after all, and I kept falling into these black holes of other people's dreams of who I should be and what I should want.

I hadn't done enough to satisfy my wild hunger for nature and creativity. The five short years since my father's death, Howard had started his own business, yet I had let my business slip away to a trickle.

Howard had said I should take the job as a school crossing guard his friend had told him about. So, I did. I loved the kids at the crossing; it was in a tough neighborhood, but I had grown up in tougher. No one liked the post because it was a crossing at a big intersection with a mix of young and older high school kids who wouldn't listen and would sometimes threaten you. The kids were rough, but for me it felt like a small piece of what I grew up in. I liked the kids, and I understood their anger and defiance. For that, I felt like I was doing something good. But I knew in my heart it wasn't my calling, and I had a hard time telling Howard I wanted to quit. I had only taken the job because Howard had asked me to. There were so many other jobs I had taken and never wanted. Office skills were important for some—something I was never good at. It seemed that no one understood what it was like to be dyslexic, and that kept me feeling ashamed and dumb while drowning in a career I didn't want.

I wanted to paint, travel, hike, and be in nature.

By trying to be a conformist and pleasing everyone there came a realization that I could express myself in my art, while I was a mute in expressing my true feelings in words and in my life. I knew I had to keep trying. As I brushed my hair and teeth, getting ready for another busy day, I looked in the mirror. I had come face-to-face with the same truth that I had glimpsed in that self-portrait so long ago, a deep discontent that followed me around like a starving puppy.

So, I drove to the wildlife center for my first day of volunteering, ready to try something new. I loved the idea of working with wild animals, as I often felt like one myself.

I also sought counseling in order to rehabilitate the lost little girl who silently lived inside of me. Trying not to hate myself was my goal. I became more and more insecure as I made mistakes, and I hated myself for not being perfect. I wanted so badly to be a perfect wife, the perfect mother, but it was something I was never able to achieve, no matter how hard I tried.

I found an unbiased wholistic therapist who I really liked. It helped to hear an outside perspective on my life. I was told I had post-traumatic stress disorder. At first, I never considered it or knew what it was. But when I learned more about it the nightmares and insomnia and triggers suddenly made sense.

For a time, I believed I was doing the right thing for my family and that I could be happy not being me. With counseling, having someone to talk to, and working to help wildlife with their rehabilitation, I began to rebuild myself. My understanding of nature had also grown in ways I had never imagined possible, and I found what was required to feed that mongrel on my first day at the nature center.

CHAPTER 9:

THE LAUGHING SQUIRREL

The doorbell rang. But I was skeptical that it was really the doorbell since I had a joker of a parrot in the house that I was bird sitting for. The African gray had become a regular as his owner, a quiet businessman, spent a lot of time in Japan.

I had learned a few words in Japanese from the bilingual bird. That part was fun.

But he was driving me and my dog crazy.

The bird would mimic the doorbell and the phone, ringing so precisely that it had become a surprise when someone was actually on the phone or at the door.

The parrot also tricked the dog, who was already dealing with a revolving door of critters that thought he was a plaything. Baby, our German shepherd, was a good nanny to the wildlife and even other dogs and feral kittens I was taking in. But this parrot seemed to have it in for my dog Baby. He would call the dog over, saying, "You-who, you-who, Baby," in a sweet I-just-want-to-love-you voice. Baby would go over to the cage to say hello. A foolish thing, because every time the parrot would bite her nose. When Baby had smartened up and refused the bird's calls, the African gray's intelligence outwitted the German shepherd's.

The bird had nothing better to do than think of ways to torture my dog, so he started to bribe her with food. He would dangle it outside the cage, then with the precise timing of a marksman, he would drop the food and bite Baby's nose! Poor Baby, she could never resist a treat, and the parrot knew it!

The parrot was just one of many crazy critters that came and went in my house. It was hard to believe how I had gotten to that point. It was like I'd hopped on a runaway train, a Noah's Ark of wayward animals. I started out rescuing unwanted and abused dogs, feral cats and kittens, and I found them good, loving homes. It felt amazing to help. Then people I knew started bringing over other unwanted and neglected pets. I had a ferret that had lost the use of his back legs because he was never allowed out of a too-small cage. Then the pet shop where I had bought all my supplies said they had customers looking for pet sitters. Most of them were parrots.

Mary, the director of the sanctuary where I trained, helped me earn my wildlife rehabilitator's license, which lead to me having orphaned wildlife at home with my two children.

Mary was an inspiration, working all day, every day doing what she loved. I had a long way to go. Even when doing things I loved part time, like taking in orphaned wildlife and working on painting, it was hard to get comfortable and give myself permission to go all the way. Something had happened, but I didn't know what it was that was holding me back. My hopes of earning a degree had been put on hold even longer, always getting delayed, and I was making it harder on myself by taking on so much. But I couldn't help myself.

Because I left working as a school crossing guard, I said yes to pet sitting, partly because of the extra money but mostly because I loved animals, and it allowed me to be home more for the girls. The animals

I didn't get paid for I took in because seeing them suffer or be without love was unbearable. When the girls and Howard came home, they never knew what new critter they would find—a hawk sitting on a dining room chair, a fox pup with a tummy ache, a crazy parrot, song birds, rabbits, and so on. While I was glad they loved animals, they didn't love them the same way I did.

By late September, hurricanes and tropical storms in the Atlantic Basin were returning, and I had released all the orphaned wildlife I had raised over the summer. Songbirds, a morning dove, the Eastern cottontail, a goose were all set free, and the house became quiet.

There is nothing I like more than a good thunderstorm. It almost seemed necessary, as if Mother Nature was cleaning her house. But the really big storms, like hurricanes, were always a source of stress.

It was the day after such a fierce storm that turned lives upside down, and I knew there would be at least a phone call or two about injured or orphaned wildlife.

We had moved inland, away from the beach I loved, and I missed being so close and taking spontaneous walks in the sand.

Also, I had learned after waking to our den filled with water that our house had been built on swampland, and we had to constantly deal with flooding and move our cars to higher ground.

That morning after the storm I went out early to see the damage in the surrounding neighborhoods, and I had taken the girls with me for a drive, followed by a walk on the beach.

It was always a thrill to stand at the edge of the sea on the land that sustained me. It amazed me to look out at the vast, mysterious, powerful ocean. I had to see with my own eyes the contrast between the land and sea; the land being so vulnerable to the weather. Afterward, only the ocean foam at the water's edge, like a rabid dog, indicated that it had awoken. I watched the waves coming and going like a breath, undamaged, powerful as ever. It was breathtaking.

After I dropped Melissa at her friend's house for the day, Julianne and I went home.

My volunteer work at the nature center refueled my spirits and brought me great joy.

But that summer with my newly acquired wildlife rehabilitator's license, I got a bit crazy. Whenever an injured critter or baby fell from a tree, I took it in but thought with summer over that I was done for the season. But that day after the hurricane, I braced myself for at least a few calls but hoped there would be none.

But there was—just one.

So when I heard the doorbell ring that day, I looked at the parrot, unsure if it was him or not. I went to the door just in case. Part of the problem was my hearing was never good, and I had no sense of direction of sound. But I was expecting someone to drop off a baby squirrel that had been found under a fallen tree. Julianne had taken the call while I was cleaning the water from the flooded den.

When I opened the door, I was surprised to see a couple standing there. They looked to be around my age, thirty or so. The husband was holding a small box.

"Hello," I said with a smile. I wanted them to feel welcome and thank them for caring enough to drop off the baby squirrel.

They smiled back but looked past me into the house.

Strange, I thought. *Do they want to come in?*

They must have seen the confused look on my face. Most of the time I would go pick up the wildlife, and sometimes they would drop them off, but either way it was often a quick hello and goodbye. Looking embarrassed, the man said, "I'm sorry, but we were hoping to meet Julianne." The woman nodded. "Is she here?" He handed me the box. It felt empty.

It must be really tiny, I thought, to weigh nothing. *Why do they want to meet my daughter?*

"You see," he explained, "she answered the phone when we called about the squirrel. She told me to find a small box and fill it with paper towels to keep it warm and bring it over as soon as we could."

"Oh," I replied, laughing. I had forgotten that she had taken the call. "Yeah, she's my little apprentice. She loves animals."

"Well, I told my wife, and she couldn't believe it was a little kid on the phone."

I giggled with pride. "Yes, she's amazing." I turned and called out for Julianne.

She came trotting out of her room. "What, Ma?"

"Come down here. Someone that wants to meet you."

She ran down the stairs with her blonde pigtails bobbing, then stood by my side. I put my free hand on her shoulder and looked in her eyes.

"These are the nice people who saved the squirrel. They wanted to meet you."

"Oh, hi," she said. "Did you have any trouble finding our house?"

They giggled and looked at each other with huge smiles on their faces, surprised to see that she was only seven years old. "Well, I told my wife how helpful and knowledgeable you were, and we wanted to meet you, Julianne."

I could see by Julianne's big grin that she was flattered.

"Thank you for your great advice on what to do."

"That's okay," she said looking up at me. I knew by the look in her eyes she wanted to go back upstairs. "Thanks, sweetie."

She said goodbye and ran back to her room.

"Well, that was something," the man said looking at his wife and sighing.

She laughed and said, "Yeah, didn't believe him when he said a little kid answered the phone and talked like an adult, never mind knowing what to do!"

"Well, she has been around them a lot lately and loves them and has apparently been paying attention to everything. Even how to get to our house!" I laughed.

We said our goodbyes, and I closed the door and called Julianne back down.

"Let's see what we got here. And, by the way, Mommy's proud of you. But next time call me down to the phone, and don't give out the address without asking, please."

"I know, you told me already," she said with a roll of her eyes.

The squirrel was so small, and with so many trees down and all the craziness of the weather, it was a miracle he was even found.

He was hairless, his skin a soft pink, and he was the size of my thumb. Both his ears and eyes were shut. Julianne watched as I warmed, hydrated, and fed him, then we named the baby squirrel before I put him in a homemade nest lined with newspaper ads and the softest toilet paper. I checked on him like a nervous, new mother would; if Chi-Chi could survive the first few nights, he could make it to adulthood.

Later, while cooking dinner, I looked out the kitchen window and could see the morning dove I had released trying to get into the bird feeder with no success. He was there every day trying, and I admired him for not giving up. Some of the thirty birds I had raised that summer were released just outside my door. The mockingbird loved to sing. He would sit in the tree outside my bedroom window and sing all night long. I would open the window and thank him and tell him how wonderful he was. Then I'd ask if he was tired and tell him he should get some rest so our family could get some sleep.

I thought Chi-Chi was just another gray squirrel to raise and release. Most of which I did at the sanctuary. There would be no thankyous, no hugs, no goodbye kisses, they would just run off and up a tree. That was the way it was supposed to be, and I was okay with that.

But Chi-Chi was different. He loved me, and that was as unexpected as my love for him.

When Chi-Chi finally opened his eyes they were so expressive and warm. Like little black diamonds that sparkled with excitement for life.

Playing like a carefree child, he seemed to enjoy life to the fullest. Although I didn't trust myself and my instincts, he trusted me and his completely. While I expected nothing from him, he gave me all of himself in the way he "spoke" to me. I tried my best to figure out what the sounds meant and worked on learning his language and customs.

A part of me wanted to believe Dr. Doolittle was real, and I was curious to know what it was like to be a squirrel, to be Chi-Chi, who was such a curious individual.

Although others didn't share in the wonderers of Chi-Chi and the pleasure I found in his company, I found talking to people about squirrels was like talking politics or religion. Everyone was passionate and had picked a side. They either loved them or hated them, and everyone had a story about a squirrel encounter. Mostly, they thought of them as pests. Sure, I had my own pesky squirrel stories about them eating and destroying my bird feeders, but the squirrels had a right to live here as much as we did.

I wanted Chi-Chi to be all that a squirrel could be, but not a pest. Chi-Chi was better than that. I knew in my heart that he would be a good member of the squirrel family.

So far, everything had gone smoothly. He was growing big and full of wonder.

He surprised me one day as we played. I chased him around and caught him on the couch. I had a sectional at the time; it was pastel blue, white, and slightly gray. Chi-Chi would run behind the pillows and then pop his head up like a little jack-in-the-box. He would let me catch him. Was it to build my confidence, or did he just want a belly rub? I turned him upside down and tickled him, and then the unexpected happened.

He laughed.

It shocked me.

I didn't know a squirrel could laugh. Then I did it again, and I laughed with him. But his sounded more like a giggle. I didn't know squirrels were even ticklish. I thought I'd learned so much about the biology of animals and their environments, but science books and magazines I had read spoke nothing of the fun, the emotions, and individual personalities of animals. It got me curious about how and why and if Chi-Chi was an anomaly. But in the end, I didn't really care since he was happy, and that made me happy.

To me, this made him unique. He was smart and adventurous.

As the days grew shorter and the leaves dropped, you could feel the cool, gray skies of fall under your skin. On the ground, orange and red hues were scattered like torn tissue paper.

November had come around fast, and our time together was coming to an end. I had to let him go before winter set in. It was almost Thanksgiving when I took Chi-Chi outside, preparing him to live on his own. If I didn't do it now, he would have to stay until spring.

Chi-Chi was off the bottle and eating food and ready to be released. We had plenty of squirrels in my neighborhood, and I thought since it was so late in the season it would be a good idea to just let him out my front door.

I poured the steaming-hot water over my English tea bag into my favorite mug. It became my ritual to have afternoon tea in honor of the grandmother I never met. She was Irish and English. I wanted to experience the feeling of being a refined English woman who drank tea at four o'clock every day with dry biscuits like I had imagined her doing.

But still I felt anything but refined with my heavy Brooklyn ascent and lack of biscuits. Though that afternoon tea was a way to be close to a woman I would never know.

Chi-Chi sat on my shoulder, and the girls were by my side as we walked out the door and through the crisp, colorful leaves that crunched like potato chips.

We had been going outside every afternoon in my yard, hot tea in hand, for weeks. My daughters would entertain themselves riding their bikes down the quiet street or "digging to China" on the side of the house.

The tree I picked out for Chi-Chi to live in was a good, strong tree. No other critter lived there, and it was close to the house, so I thought it would be a good place for Chi-Chi to live.

"Okay," I said, "here we go."

I released him, and he went up and down the tree, then up and down my leg to the top of my head, showing off. Did he think I would chase him?

"Sorry, Chi-Chi, I was never good at climbing."

I looked around to see if there were any other squirrels, but there were none to be found. Chi-Chi and I walked around and played some more, and then I sat in the chair I had placed under the tree, next to a stash of wood being seasoned and used on a cold winter night, not for the heat but for the mesmerizing glow of the untouchable flames. Baby was busy piling up sticks she had found next to the woodpile. She had seen us pick up the pieces of wood and stack them and thought she could help. Melissa joined in, though the days of "I love you, Mommy" and hugs and kisses had faded away to teen rebellion, and I was enemy number one. Even if it was only for a moment, watching Melissa and Chi-Chi play hide-and-seek brought back memories of my little girl.

I had my ideas about where he should live and, like any independent child growing up, Chi-Chi had his idea of where *he* wanted to live. I picked the tree, he picked the woodpile.

He began collecting leaves and disappearing into the woodpile with them. Whenever he came out, he would get more and disappear again. This went on for a week. As the sun started to go down, Chi-Chi would climb up on my shoulder, and as we headed into the house, he would curl up for a nap while I made dinner.

The big day had come, as I knew it would. But I wanted it to be his decision, not mine. Chi-Chi had decided it was time. I had called my daughters in and gotten up from my chair, the book I was reading still in my hand, the sun fading away. The lights in my house had lured me inside to the warmth of cooking, cleaning, checking homework, and doing laundry.

If I was lucky and not too exhausted, maybe after midnight I could sneak in to my studio for a few hours of painting. I saw Chi-Chi sitting on the ground next to the woodpile and called for him. He only stared at me with those big, round eyes, his tail fluffed and pointing up, curled like a question mark. I knew what he was saying the moment I looked into his eyes. He wouldn't be coming inside with me tonight. He was a big boy now, all grown up, and he had made his home in the woodpile.

I told him I'd be right next door if he needed me, then I walked away, looking back just in case he changed his mind. The weather was good, although chilly, and I had no idea what would happen or if he would be afraid to be alone. But he wanted to go, so I walked away. That night I worried about him and kept looking out the window, wondering how he was.

Then It started snowing! *Oh no*, I thought. He had picked some night to be a free spirit.

I was still kind of new to being a wildlife rehabilitator and was cautioned about imprinting, which is a way of learning who you are as a species. When an animal or bird is born, it identifies with its parents. Birds do this visually after hatching, and when humans raise animals, there is a risk that the animal will not recognize its own species, and then it's not safe to be released back into the wild, as they will seek out humans.

So far, I didn't have any that thought they were human. I was the mom, and they had come to me, but when they saw another human outside my family, they would hide or run away, and after I released them, they were wild, and it made me a proud, wild mother.

They walked and flew when I let them go, not once turning back to say goodbye to the one who had mothered them. This is the way it was supposed to be. Yet it was still hard to let go, and I felt ashamed for wanting more. I was used to caring for dogs and cats, and all I had to do was make a phone call to find out how they were in their new homes, and I could even go visit if I desired. It was different with wild animals. Except for the handful of birds I had released in the yard I would never know what happened to the others.

Chi-Chi would change that. There were no bags for Chi-Chi to pack, only leaves he collected for his rent-free room in a woodpile.

Some children who leave home for the first time can find life isn't perfect and return with a heavy heart. The confidence they had left with being momentarily lost, and it would take the comforts of home and mothering to bring it back.

The next morning it was early and the air was crisp when I opened the front door to check out the season's first snow. I looked down, and there he was. On top of his head, my little Chi-Chi had a perfect little part in his fur.

How long had he been sitting there, waiting for someone to open the door?

Did he want his mother or his safe bed in the warm house? Had I failed him?

I frowned, but then I couldn't help but smile at his new look.

I opened the door all the way to let him in.

He looked like a worn-out alfalfa from the little rascals.

"I'm sorry," I said.

He looked up at me, defeat in his eyes. He walked past me with his head hung low. His usual bouncy, gliding gait was gone.

I knew that walk of defeat; I had done it so many times myself.

I could only imagine what had happened on his first night out in the world. He had proudly curled up in his new home that he had built, and for his troubles, he got the water torture with a slow drip on his head all night.

Now he had returned to his mother after he thought he was an independent, self-sufficient man. He walked past me to the cage he had called home for so long. I followed him. He climbed in and settled down, wrapping his tail around him, sighed, and closed his eyes. He slept most of the day, and when he woke up, he stretched and groomed himself. The unnatural part the water had made in his fur was gone. He ate and then went to the door, turning to me as if to say, *I'm ready, Mom.* As he went outside, I closed the door and watched from my window as not to interfere. He toiled in the snow-covered leaves.

His mouth filled with leaves he carried them over, then disappeared in the woodpile to plug up the hole in the roof of his new home. Despite the setback and fatigue, he picked himself up and went back into the big world to live as a free-spiritized, laughing squirrel.

I never fed him, and he never came in the house again. When I went outside, he still occasionally climbed up to my shoulder for a hello and a tickle. Chi-Chi had the confidence he needed and looked so sure of himself. He was wild and had a strange mother who walked on two legs and didn't have a tail. I contemplated what the other squirrels would say to him if they knew. I was a proud squirrel mom and working hard to become the artist I wanted to be, and I had Chi-Chi to thank for reminding me.

As I was reflecting on him and my own defeats, I realized that if he could do it, then I could too. I went back into my studio with what that sweet little squirrel had given me—the confidence to not give up on my dreams of being a full-time artist.

CHAPTER 10:

THE AFFAIR

It was a quiet morning as Mary and I sat hunched down in a blind looking up at the sky. I had been going to meet her at the beach whenever I could for the last two fall seasons. We had set up the mist nets and blind close to the dunes just as the sun rose.

We both perked up when we saw a speck in the sky headed our way. Then she slumped down with disappointment.

"No," Mary said. "It's just a sapsucker."

I looked at her with puzzlement and disbelief of how she could tell what kind of bird it was from so far away.

"How can you tell? I could never do that."

Mary said, "JoAnne, you can learn anything if you want to. You'll know them all, even from far away, you just need to learn their giss, which is the impression of a bird. When looking at its features in flight you notice its shape, the way they fly, size, coloration, habitual movements, and its call, combined with its habitat and location. Those kind of things"

I took in every word as I watched her eyes dart around. She reminded me of a fox in the brush waiting for its prey to fly into its open mouth.

"Habitual? What does that mean?"

Mary never took her eyes off the sky. She was so focused, so serious, like when she spoke at the sanctuary.

"Habitual." She paused, then glanced over to me. "It's like...a habit, something they do over and over. It's the way they fly. That's how I knew it wasn't a hawk."

"I really don't think I can do that," I mumbled.

My heart sunk. As much as I thought I had grown, I still had doubts about my skills.

I took a deep breath, knowing I had to work more on my self-loathing.

Mary and I sat there for well over an hour before we caught a bird. It was fortunate, as some days we would be there for hours with no luck at all.

We rushed out of our hiding place to see. Then carefully removed him from the mist net. It was windy and cold, and I was shivering and tired but excited to see what we had caught.

"This one's special," Mary said, excited.

"What is it?"

"It's a peregrine falcon."

It was the first time I had ever seen one. He was beautiful with his black head that fell like a teardrop into the white. He was a warrior, an explorer of the skies. But he already had a band on his leg. He had been captured before. I wondered why he didn't learn from the first time. I guess I wasn't the only one who needed more than one lesson on how to stay out of trouble.

In that moment I could feel the power of the wild. I wanted to take a piece of that wildness home with me while also sending that part of me away with him.

I had Mary, the director of the nature center, to thank for teaching me about birds. It was with her that I connected with this world-traveling bird, something I wished I could be.

We collected data for further understanding of a bird's life and travels, after researching the origin of the band number on the peregrine falcon we'd caught and released.

Mary had told me that that one flew all the way from Denmark.

"Wow," I exclaimed, because the idea turned my brain upside down. It was hard to believe a bird could fly all the way to Long Island from a place so far away and foreign to me.

I wanted to know more so I borrowed books on birds of prey from the sanctuary's small library. I fell in love with what I learned was the fastest bird in the world. I had a newfound passion and respect for the peregrine. They hunted, as all birds of prey do, with their binocular vision high up in the sky. When they spot their prey, the peregrine spirals down in a corkscrew pattern to not lose sight of the target. Peregrine falcons had been making a comeback from the pesticide DDT and from the endangered-species list. I felt a kinship with the bird as I was trying not to lose sight of my target, my goal. Which was getting my bachelor's degree in fine art and having a real career.

But Howard never wanted to go to a museum or to the sanctuary, only to a bar or to look at cars. I would go with him and then alone to the galleries and sometimes on the weekends with the girls. Howard did, for a while, go hiking with us. There were some happy, though short-lived, family moments, but it took so much effort to get him to go, and those moments were falling away, replaced by many more nights out with friends. Something he always did, but now bars and pool halls and coming home later and later became the norm while I was busy at home cooking, cleaning, going over homework, taking care of animals, and painting when I could.

I felt he wanted a single life and was acting on it. There was a big part of me that was old school Roman Catholic Italian where divorce wasn't to be considered. But It was the girls who caused me to pause on the idea, and I would had given it to him if he had ever asked. I also offered it up, but he had said no. I was confused about why he wanted to be in our marriage, and I let the offensive feeling sit with me, trying to make it work by ignoring the obvious.

My girls still believed in me—well, at least one of them.

I craved more time to sleep in. It was like that most times now, hard to face the day. But my time at the sanctuary kept me going. And on one of those spring mornings before I went to volunteer, I found Melissa, my teenage daughter, was already up. She, like her father and my mother, was part of the "morning-people clan." I was not and was reminded often by my mother, who would call early, and Howard that it was wrong to be anything but happy to get up early. But for me, a lifelong insomniac, I stumbled out of bed and into Julianne's room to take a deep breath. She wasn't a morning person either. "Honey, it's time to get up," I said with a sigh.

Twenty minutes and five trips up and down the stairs later: "You *really* need to get up! You'll miss the bus."

She complied with a nod.

I understood and said, "It's too bad they don't have afternoon school for people like us. I laid your clothes out for you and made you some oatmeal and packed your lunch."

I ran back downstairs to argue with Melissa about eating something before she went to school. She wanted cold pizza. "Pizza has protein, Ma. You said I needed some protein." She used my words against me.

"Missy, please, no pizza for breakfast."

I had made eggs for Howard, who was gone to work before the kids came down. I no longer made him lunches with notes written on napkins. So, I thought he didn't like them and stopped putting them in. He never acknowledged them, and now he ate out for lunch every day.

I did still do that for the girls, but Mellissa seamed more embarrassed by them now that she was in junior high. I would draw a heart with arrows and smiley faces. Always, *I love you, and have a great day!* But it felt like no one seemed to care that I loved them. I had to remind myself that Julianne was still young and the only one who appreciated the notes and me. But I also was painfully aware that a day would come where I would fall from grace in her eyes, and she would see me for the flawed woman I was. These were the fears and insecurities I carried around—aware but helpless to remove, as it was like trying to run away from your shadow.

After the girls left for school and I was alone in the kitchen trying to muster enthusiasm for cleaning the morning mess, the phone rang. I was still always surprised to hear someone there as the bird that mimicked the phone had left his imprint on me. It was Mary from the nature center. Mary had no reason to call me, as I didn't think we were that kind of friends, assuming that I was just one of the many volunteers at the sanctuary, not anyone special enough to call.

"I have something for you. Can you come in early today?"

"I think so. What is it?"

"It's a surprise."

Hum. A surprise? I love surprises!

"Okay, I'll head over now," I said.

I hung up. I'd have to hurry down to the sanctuary before the kids came home from school, and the laundry and dishes would just have to wait.

When I got on the parkway, I turned up the music and stepped on the gas. It was my time, and I was determined to drive away from the voices in my head telling me that I didn't deserve to have joy in my life. That I should be doing something else. There had been a steady stream of dull jobs that I'd taken, endless laundry and dishes to clean. Working as a waitress, a short-order cook, a hostess, a cashier, dishwasher, babysitter, in an office, as a school crossing guard, in an advertising house as a typesetter, transporting and driving trucks, making Mardi Gras masks and hand-painted clothing, an animal sitter, animal trainer, and more jobs than I could even remember. But never a full-time artist.

The feeling of guilt for not being satisfied with a job or a kitchen had been overwhelming. Why couldn't I just be grateful for not having to go to the laundromat anymore or that we had a house and a phone and food on the table?

My open window let the guilt and question of why I wasn't happy fly out as the music started playing and the wheels of the car turned. It was time to shut it all down and just ride.

I knew what I was doing wasn't wrong, but it felt like I was having a secret affair.

The secret was my desire for freedom from my racing brain and restless soul. It wasn't freedom from my family. I loved them and would do anything for them. This little affair I was having on my own with nature and new people. *My* people. It quieted the volcano of emotions and dissatisfaction with myself and my marriage that had been falling apart before it began.

I wasn't hiding where I was going, and I wanted to share it with my husband. But we were different people, and maybe we always had been, but I didn't want to believe it.

I parked the car and got out and smiled as I took a deep breath.

When I stepped through the gates of the sanctuary it was like passing into a realm of new possibilities, a place where I felt my reason for existence was accessible. Being surrounded by trees created this sensation. Was it the abundance of oxygen or the energy of a peaceful forest?

It could have been. But I wasn't thinking about such things. I was drunk on nature; it felt good, and there was no need to think.

Nature became my new sacred place, my church.

Like my time spent painting and drawing, it allowed me to feel like there were endless possibilities for the life I desired. For these moments in time, I was free of all inhibitions and self-deprecating thoughts.

This feeling was especially prevalent when I entered the wildlife sanctuary. The fountain just inside the gate would trigger this, as the clock striking twelve on a Sunday would trigger the chimes and bells on the church steeple.

The sanctuary fountain was a beautiful, delicate, life-sized sculpture of a barefoot girl with curls draping down. Her flowing dress pressed against her indicating an unforeseen breeze. She looked down as she held up a tray overflowing with water that trickled into a circular stone pond. Its sound mimicked a slow-running stream.

In front of the girl was a young boy who sat relaxed, his bare feet hanging over the rocks, fully focused on the bird who had just landed on his hand. On the side of the boy, tucked away, was a squirrel who seemed content and connected to the children. There was a second bird behind the girl at her feet. The birds mimicked each other with wings forever frozen open.

It was a balanced, serene scene cast in bronze. I wanted to have been that happy girl. I also wished I was the artist who had created the sculpture.

It was what I had always looked for.

Harmony.

Harmony in my life, for mankind, nature, and the woman I knew I could be. It was the thing missing in my home.

The forest was mighty, mysterious, and full of wonderful creatures that I longed to know.

When I arrived at the sanctuary, I took in the sunshine. The smells of honeysuckle mixed with pine and the cacophony of sounds created a cocktail that filled my senses, a symphony of songbirds singing a spring tune. The light dappled and danced on the ground as the trees swayed on the shady walkway. I was so in love.

As I walked past the pond laden with green algae, it made me think of the new controversy that had been brewing between the local botanist and director of the sanctuary, who liked the algae and felt it was part of nature. The botanist wanted to remove it and put in water lilies. "We control enough in the world," was Mary's response, and as director she had the final say, leaving the botanist with a small chip on her shoulder.

I didn't have an opinion about it and kept my head down, trying to look busy when the subject came up; I was just happy to be there.

I was ready to scrub the pans and clean out the aviaries and even feed the rats that I used to dread seeing as a child. It was a challenge for me to be around such creatures. Seeing them brought up old resentments—for the invasion of my childhood home and the nightly fear of them coming to bite me in my sleep.

One in particular would greet the visitors and was friends with the receptionist. The rat bonded with her, and her with him. He would spend the day scurrying back and forth from the edge of the desk, stealing little bits of paper and making its nest behind the telephone. I suppose since he couldn't answer the phone, he had to do something to look busy.

I wanted to make peace with this species and felt I was making progress by saying hello to the rats. It was the best I could do and was ecstatic that I didn't have to clean out their cages. Instead, I was to clean out the aviaries, feeding the birds and doing "artistic" research that took me on exploratory walks and bird-banding expeditions.

My purpose there was to help these wild creatures who had already had so much to contend with. The least I could do was keep their new home clean. I was grateful for helping them, and in return they helped calm my racing mind.

Also, unlike my people at home, people here had thanked me for cleaning and my work as an artist. There wasn't a single snide remark or put-down. But even if there was, I would have done all of it anyway because of the wild animals I felt akin to. It was nice to hear a thank you and to feel appreciated.

When I arrived, I stopped to say hello to the new arrivals.

A peregrine falcon arrived who sadly would never fly again. He had great stature and an intriguing look in his eyes. In their dissent they could reach up to seventy miles an hour. But in the modern world of power lines that didn't fit into their evolution, they would sometimes run into them at full speed and fall to the ground, helpless and confused, never to fly again.

This injured one had come into the sanctuary with a lost wing and became a permanent resident. Fascinating that I could still see all the pride and dignity of a great warrior in his dark eyes. I had to paint him. On his good side, of course, wings intact, with my paintbrush. After the visitors left, I would take him into the building and set him on a perch to study him closer. In my work as an artist painting wildlife, the most important thing to me, and the thing I started with, was the eyes. You didn't have to speak the same language or be the same species to communicate and understand, all you had to do was look into their eyes. That's where the whole story is, and that's where I would start.

I wished I could have painted him a new wing so he could be free and fly home. But all I could do was feed him and keep his new home clean.

I wanted to hold the wildlife forever on canvas so I could save the moment and honor these beings gifted with the magic of flight.

As I painted him, I could still see the glory of the great bird he once was. It reminded me of the photos I had seen of the American Indians, even though they had lost their land, yet never their dignity. You could see it in the portraits of them. It was in their eyes, no matter what the body said. The truth of the being is always in the eyes.

I wanted to imagine for the falcon that nothing was ever lost and one day he'd be free. I pondered if he would ever feel any sense of freedom in his new aviary. It was built tall and wide for the birds to fly, something he would never do. It made me question what freedom meant. It was something I often thought about as I had never felt free myself.

I looked the word up. The dictionary states that *freedom* means "not subject to or constrained by engagements or obligations." But that's a human point of view. What of this bird's point of view? I wish I could have asked him. Was he or anyone or anything free any longer, and were we ever really free? Is freedom just a state of mind? Everything seems constrained and limited, whether by obligation or engagement.

Obligation—was it a choice? Are we obligated to others and the living things of nature are obligated to each other; it's a symbiotic flow of our planet and universe. But we're limited by constraints that are self-inflicted and at times imposed by others.

Because of obligations and constraints, it seemed like a fantasy to be free.

The word and concept of *wild* and *free* go hand in hand. If we say something is wild, then are we also saying that it's free? I wanted to know. But how could I?

The thought of the peregrine falcon followed me home, and I took my time painting every feather, and when I'd finished the painting, it was like finishing a good book or movie. I had enjoyed the time spent with it. Sad that it was over but glad I saw it to the end. I kept the painting and still look at it every day as a reminder that we may sometimes be damaged but will never be broken. I would feed that falcon and the other birds of prey with remorse for their new life. I was also working on painting native wildflower signs for the wooded trails.

As part of my research for the trail signs I took walks with the local botanist, who rattled off names of plants and their medicinal purposes like an auctioneer taking bids. We would sometimes picnic or go to her house for lunch and even paint together. She would occasionally bring up the top of the unwanted algae. I would change the subject.

I did very much like her. Nancy was much older than me and so different from anyone I knew. She came from old money and had a beautiful old house on the edge of a nature preserve that her family had donated to the town. But that's not what I liked about her. She was kind and full of energy, and I had a great respect for her knowledge. She loved plants and nature. We were from completely different backgrounds but came together for the goals of—conservation, art, and maintaining a natural world.

I was like a sponge, trying to absorb everything that she and Mary said as I held on to the mental images of all the species of plants and trees and birds in all their phases of life. It surprised me how much I remembered and how much fun I had painting them.

It felt good that I was leaving my mark at the sanctuary. Not a timeless wonder, just a fleeting one. Visitors passed my wooden sign that hung under an old tree on the way into the aviary. The painting was of a red-tailed hawk, pointing toward the birds-of-prey enclosures.

I was proud of it, and it was a thing I felt when I left—a small piece of me was still there. It wasn't uncommon for me to take an animal that needed special care home for the night.

Howard seemed to at least like the animals I brought home as much as the girls.

It made me giddy inside to tell him that I was doing research for painting. Something I don't think he liked very much since I spent so much time and money going to art school.

It made me feel like a child asking for permission from my husband to do the things I loved. I felt like he would tolerate it as long as it didn't interfere too much with my homework and bringing in an income. At home, it felt as if I was just a servant.

It was a lot to do and balance, but it was worth it because I could be myself around the animals and people who shared the love of nature and all its diversity.

After I made my presence known, Mary called me into her office. I didn't know what all the secrecy was about on the phone, and I was anxious to find out. I loved surprises.

Even though I knew that Mary had something good to tell me— maybe an art show? Some new wild animal that I would get to see for the first time?—it was the negativity in me and a lifetime of disappointment that peeked behind the curtain of hope and joy and whispered in my ear, *She doesn't want you here anymore. She's going to tell you to go home because even though you're only volunteering and not getting paid, you'll still be fired.*

I swallowed hard and pushed the thoughts out. That kind of thinking would only hurt me. They were mean-spirited beasts, and I was still trying to tame them.

She was smiling, just as I had seen her in my mind on the phone earlier that morning. I smiled back and sighed with relief. Then thought about the dishes still in the sink from breakfast and felt a pinch of guilt for being at the sanctuary instead of at home. I was a bad person for leaving dishes in the sink.

When I moved to speak, she put her finger to her lips for me to be quiet.

She whispered and pointed to a shoebox on the floor. She pulled out her leather gloves and put them on. I knew by the shape of the box that it wasn't a hawk. But what could possibly be in a shoebox that she would need leather gloves for? Not a squirrel or a baby bird. It couldn't have been a fox. It was feeling like the guessing game you played when you were a child, when you had to wait to open a present. The giver of that present could hardly wait and wanted you to guess.

Is it bigger than a bread box? Today you would have to explain what a bread box was, and even the use of the word *bread box* would need an explanation.

This was going to be fun.

CHAPTER 11:

MISCHIEF-MAKERS

As I hovered over the mystery box on the floor of Mary's small, cluttered office, I felt like a child waiting for a surprise. Near Mary's desk was a young blue jay. He hopped over to the corner of his cage to get a closer look at the box. Likewise, I leaned forward with anticipation.

The cage sat next to the paper-filled desk with the phone that often rang. The blue jay had learned to speak and would repeatedly say hello and then screech. His screech mimicked the vocal red-tailed hawk who lived in the aviary an earshot away.

But he and the phone were quiet now, watching as we sat cross-legged with the shoebox between us. We were all staring at it like Cub Scouts mesmerized at a campfire.

The room vanished, as I was completely captivated by what was in the box. She lifted the cardboard top off as if it was made of fragile glass. All I saw inside were a pile of paper towels. She slowly pealed back the paper towels and kept looking up for my reaction. Although I didn't know why, it was clear she wanted to see it through my eyes.

Curled up, sound asleep, was a live ball of gray fur not much bigger than the stuffed animal it was holding on to. It could have fit in the palm of my hand. When Mary nudged the living furball, I finally realized what it was—a baby racoon. He snarled at her like a grumpy old bear being woken from a winter sleep. What a fierce sound!

Being so small, and possibly dealing with humans for the first time, he must have been terrified.

Mary looked in my eyes. She was so genuine, and I knew at that moment she had become a true friend. Her voice softened. She opened up, and I felt her true heart.

"I know that you love mammals," she said. "My love is for birds, mostly birds of prey. I know you'll take good care of him."

She looked down at the baby in the box. She was almost whispering when she said, "I wanted you to raise him. But be careful, he's still a wild animal who's alone and has lost his mother. He can still bite."

I was saddened by the fact that he was taken away from his natural environment and by the loss of his mother. I imagined him hovering over his mother's body and touching her. I saw him in deep despair and confusion. But I really didn't know the details of how he had become an orphan. Now his life was in the hands of what he must have thought of as aliens.

As I headed to the car with the shoebox, I thought about what had just happened. Mary had a way with hawks and falcons that was beyond me. She was right that I loved birds, but I understood mammals and had a way with them. It seemed to me as if Mary could see into my restless, tortured soul and wanted to ease my pain. She somehow knew that by giving me the challenge of helping this baby, I would also be helped in some way.

But how could she know? I pondered as I put the shoebox on the front seat of my car and turned off the radio. She knew so little about my life and I so little about hers outside of our love for animals.

When I got home Baby's ears perked up when she smelled the box. I took it into my art/rehab studio. It was a small spare bedroom I used as an art studio and had become a wildlife nursery for the newbies, and he was the first of this season.

I sat down and fed him his first bottle. Just like a baby he wrapped his warm, soft, little hands around my finger, and I fell in love. He had melted my heart. It has always been interesting to me to see what we all have in common. Human nature and the diversity of wildlife.

I wondered what I might have in common with this little guy. Racoons had often been thought of as mischievous, hated for their nightly runs on neighborhood garbage cans. Raccoons, I thought, were just out to see what the world had to offer and felt they were perhaps just as misunderstood as I was. Figuring out what to name him took no time at all. I thought of *I Love Lucy*, and if he had been a girl, I would have named him Lucy, for she was surely a mischief-maker, but the next best thing was Ricky. It was also fun to say Ricky the Racoon.

Ricky was like having a newborn. And just like my own babies, I waited until he fell asleep and tucked him in, then tried to sneak away to bed. But he must have had the hearing of Superman, because I swear, I didn't make a sound, yet he still noticed.

Ricky cried out, and I ran back to comfort him.

Boy, was I in trouble. It was all I could do not to get overly attached.

Nevertheless, one of my biggest concerns was that the wildlife I rehabbed or released would become a pest and turn on humans. It's something I tried to avoid at all costs.

Making sure there was nothing Ricky could get into, I crawled around the floor to see from Rickey's point of view. I did this before when my children were babies; doing it for a raccoon, it might look a little strange.

Ricky followed me around the house and then the yard, but he always whined and chirped like a little bird when he went back in his home, and that made it hard for me not to give in. He was so sweet and cute and most of the time no trouble at all.

This sweetness cast a spell, and I had forgotten all about the cleverness of the mischievous raccoons I had read about.

When I left the house, I put Ricky in his encloser. He complained but soon seemed to settle down.

Only Ricky was much more observant than I had given him credit for.

I learned the hard way about raccoons' hand dexterity and insatiable curiosity.

It seemed Ricky was watching every move I made and taking notes. Did he put on his spyglasses and keep a secret little notepad and pencil somewhere in his enclosure? Maybe he hid it in the stuffed animal he slept with, waiting for the right moment to strike?

After picking up the girls from after-school activities, we went to the store and spent longer than usual buying groceries.

"Okay," I said to the girls, "a half hour of TV, then homework. What would you like as a snack?"

The grocery bags still in my hands, I put the key in the door, opened it wide, and my jaw dropped. The kids were still behind me as I wondered where the dog was. I felt a wave of panic.

"Did someone rob us?" Melissa asked.

I said, "Stay here," and made them wait by the door while I cautiously looked around hoping whoever broke in had gone.

My heart was pounding when I entered the kitchen. The cabinets were all open, the cereal, sugar, and flour was all over the floor.

Moving through the house, the girls followed in my footsteps, and I turned and whispered, "No, keep back. Wait while I check it out."

I turned around. "Hello-hello? Is anybody there?" I wondered and worried where Baby was. I followed the cyclone of a mess through the house into the den, then the laundry room. The powdered laundry detergent was all over the floor. So was the laundry. It was then I found the culprit, the mess-maker.

The whole thing caught me off guard, having totally forgotten that I had a raccoon in my house! Ricky was in the bottom of a paper bag that was standing upright. He looked just like he did in the shoebox at the sanctuary, curled up in a ball, only this time he was bigger.

I smirked and shook my head, whispering to the girls to come over and look inside the bag, and although I never asked them, I was sure they were glad it wasn't them who made that mess and that poor Ricky was going to be in a lot of trouble. I laughed.

Baby had made herself scarce, hiding in the bedroom. She must have thought I would blame her for the mess. She was such a sensitive dog and had a lot to contend with in this house. She was subject to little girls' tea parties and reluctant nanny to a host of animals that fell in love with her. Birds biting her nose and artists painting her portrait. Feral kittens hissing and stray dogs that came and went. Now she must have thought she would get blamed for Ricky getting out of what I thought was a secure enclosure. Maybe Ricky felt like a snack and figured, "Oh, I know where the snacks are" and helped himself.

"We were outsmarted by a baby raccoon. I need a better lock on his enclosure door," I said. It would be impossible for me to be mad or blame a raccoon for being a raccoon. It made me think—if I was blaming myself for being me, then what was the cause? If I could accept Ricky for being himself and having fun doing it, then why was I always berating myself for being me? And why was I so hard on Melissa? It seemed I could be more forgiving to a raccoon than my own children or myself.

This would be something I would have to contemplate more and maybe soften myself when it came to my girls. Then, as I started to clean up, I couldn't help but remember my beautiful firstborn, Melissa, when she made her first big mess. As we put everything back, I told the girls that story.

We were young and had no money, no furniture, and had been renting a small apartment in the upstairs of a private house. It had a small kitchen and living room and two small bedrooms. We had nothing but a TV that would change channels by itself every time a plane went overhead. It was given to us by my father, who had gotten it from the hospital. We had one very old recliner that my husband and I would fight over, as we had only one other chair—a hardwood in the kitchen. No couch, just rugs over hardwood floors. Which is why we fought over the chair, but Melissa always had dibs on the chair and our laps.

We had a few plates and glasses and some silverware but ate on the floor. We bought two mattresses, a full size and a twin that sat on the floor. It worked for our little toddler because there wasn't much she could get into trouble with, but she found it anyway.

The door to Melissa's room had been shut when I walked in to check on her. We always kept the door open, and I was stunned at how quickly she made a mess. She looked like a miniature clown—all in white with big red lips in a diaper. She was shirtless and covered in baby powder. It stuck to the red lipstick on her lips and face. In her bed was her little doll that lay naked, also covered in baby powder and lipstick. Baby powder was everywhere. When I asked her about it, she acted surprised, like she didn't know what I was talking about.

"What happened? Who made this mess?" I inquired.

She looked around as if searching for someone to pin it on.

When I asked if she took out the baby powder and the lipstick, she said "No, Mommy" with the most innocent baby voice, her tiny hands raised in the air, palms up, and she had told her very first lie.

Trying not to hide my laughter, I put on my poker face, then raised my hand, as she had just done. I asked, "Well, what happened? How did the baby powder get all over you, your dolly, and the room?"

She looked around as if she had never seen her room or me before.

I tilted my head and furrowed my brow. "And is that Mommy's lipstick?

Her hands went together, and she raised her tiny index finger to her chin. She mirrored my furrowed brow and tilted head.

"Mommy," she said.

"Yes?" I said, waiting, then looked around the room as if I was confused. "How did Mommy's lipstick get on your face?" I looked over to her doll laying on her bed. I gestured and added, "And it's on your dolly's face too. Who made this big mess?" I shrugged. I knew the answer but wanted to hear her take on it. She looked so adorable, and I was immersed in the moment knowing it would always be memorable and a complete joy of my new motherhood.

I'd been in her shoes before, but I was going to handle this better than my parents had handled that with me when I did something out of innocence and exploration.

She turned to the doll and said, "The baby did it?"

Wow, I thought, *she lied with a straight face looking me right in the eyes.*

I felt the comedy of it all and couldn't help but smile.

"I don't understand?" I questioned her more.

"The baby did it?"

I saw the hope in her eyes that I was buying her story, and I was sure when she got a little older, she would try to convince me to buy the Brooklyn Bridge.

She waved her little hands about as if performing in a dramatic opera. "Oh, yes, Mommy," she exclaimed pointing to the culprit on the bed. "She did it."

Wow, you just threw that baby doll under the bus.

"Oh my!" I put my hand to my head as if I didn't know what to do. "What a bad baby, to make such a mess. What should we do?"

"I don't know, Mommy." Then she walked over to the baby. "Bad baby, bad baby."

"Well," I said, leaning down to her level, "I think it'll be okay. I think the baby is sorry. Do you think she's sorry?"

"Yes, Mommy," she answered with excitement in her voice.

"I know what," I said. "I have an idea."

She looked at me slightly concerned, so cute and covered in lipstick and baby powder.

"What do you think?" I asked "Do you think if she helps us clean up and promises not to touch Mommy's lipstick or use all the baby powder again it will be okay?"

"Yes, Mommy!" she answered, nodding.

I realized looking at Ricky that I had let the fear set in. I was afraid of my children failing and struggling in life as I had. I could see my daughters' potential and wanted the best for them. Because of this fear I became hard on Melissa as she entered her teen years, which come with raging hormones, social pressures, and split-second decisions that can be life-changing. There's an inherent curiosity for the young about life and a need to discover how things work for yourself, and sometimes there's a bit of magic and evolution in mischief. My own curiosity as a child would leave me feeling like a bad kid. Once I had taken the radio apart to see how it worked, but I couldn't figure out how to put it back together. Although I could understand why it wasn't appreciated, it made me feel like I was bad.

Ricky helped me see who I had been—just a kid who loved to explore and learn how things work. It made me wonder about parenting in other species and if a lion or wolf worries at night if they were too harsh on their children or if they're amused by their follies. Every moment leaves a mark on the paths of our understanding as humans and parents, which is only a small part of a much larger story. And if I was to evolve in my story, I had to be willing to change.

While Ricky was still young and training to be released, he became my late-night companion. At two in the morning I would take him outside and teach him how to forage for food. We would tend to our gardens, which I loved, and it turned out Ricky enjoyed them as well. He needed to learn how to live around and fear people. He needed to fit in and be a good neighbor. This was my goal and hope for him. In my experience as a parent of a wild child, I knew Ricky would need to be wild to thrive, distrustful of people, and come out at night to eat. What does a creature of the night do in suburbia?

I could see this being a problem as I was not the only one in the neighborhood with a vegetable garden, and garbage cans were abundant. But I discovered right away that Ricky loved to eat snails and slugs. Perfect! I thought this could work out. And although I liked snails and slugs, they were a big pain in the butt when it came to my flowers and vegetable garden. I refused to use pesticides, so after a weekend of barbecue and a couple beers I would take the leftover beer in little cups and tuck them under my flower and vegetable beds. But it never completely solved the problem until one night when it was late and quiet with a light mist in the air. Ricky and I slipped out the back door while everyone else slept. I wondered what he was going to eat and how we would forage in my modest backyard. As soon as we stepped outside Ricky stopped at the flowers in the pot next to the entrance of the door. His hands moved feverishly, and he seemed excited, so I bent down to see what he had found. He grumbled and ran off into the corner to eat what turned out to be a slug. I laughed, and he looked up at me with his little prize close to him as if I wanted to take it away, though I assured him I had no such intention. Sitting on the steps I shook my head and waited. After he ate his slug, he came back and gave me a nuzzle and then went back to the flower pots. I never saw another slug or snail eating my flowers or vegetables as long as Ricky, my slug superhero, was around.

Ricky's outdoor enclosure was ready, and it was time to move him outside. This was a painful process for both of us. I was an anxious mom sending her child out to the world for the first time. That night, as I had done before, I paced back and forth. I went to the window every time I heard his little chirping sounds, calling for me. I thought of the first time I had sent my girls to school, their first time on the school bus alone. I couldn't help but jump in my car and follow the bus all the way there. I parked the car on the corner like a private detective with my sunglasses on and spied on my own child. I watched as they got off the bus and went into the school. I also went back to watch them get back on the bus and followed it home. They would have been annoyed if they knew.

When Julianne caught me in the car outside her school, she asked why I was there. I told her I had to run out, which was true, but I didn't tell her why. I did that kind of thing every chance I could and tried to hide it. And I was no different with my little wild charges.

Well after everybody was in bed, I would go outside to let Ricky out. We would walk around so he could learn about the world. Each time he checked the flowerpots for slugs and snails, and we would play a game of midnight hide-and-seek. Each night he would wander further and further from me, and I became panic-stricken. My heart pulled me to be with him, and I would call out, and he would come out from an unseen place. Sometimes he was right in front of me hiding behind a tree or a shed, surprising me every time.

Then I would put him back for the night, and he would chirp just like a bird for me to come back and release him. He wanted the comfort and security of being in a comfortable home with his family. He was still too small to be on his own, but I knew he would be okay eventually and would accept living like a raccoon. I thought of his mother, how proud she would be of Ricky. He was such a handsome racoon and had a soft, beautiful coat that I loved to touch.

Once summer was coming to an end it was time. Although it took a little convincing and arguing with myself to come to that conclusion. Finally the night came, and I didn't put him back in his enclosure; I left the door open for him to come and go as he pleased. I knew it was time when he heard another voice or car he would always run and hide. He was a big boy now, and it seemed like the right moment when he started drifting further away from me and the yard. I sat down on the grass in the backyard waiting to see if he would come back. Sometimes I would even fuss with my garden. I couldn't imagine what the neighbors would think if they saw me out there at 3:00 AM preening and watering my tomatoes. But they never did, nor did they know about Ricky. Then Ricky went about his business of being a racoon in the wilds of suburbia with confidence. My calls for him went unanswered, and I thought I should go to bed.

I knew he understood that I was his mother and human, but he needed to stay away from other people, and he did. Eventually I thought he would stay away from me, but I would always miss him and wondered if he would miss me too, or would I drift away from his mind? Though my children were still young, I imagined what it would be like when they left the house and how it would differ from now. I wondered if I could cope with it.

My main goal was to teach my wild and biological children to be independent and self-reliant. I wanted my children to have a good life and be happy, and I hoped they would still want me around when they left the nest. But who wants their mom around all the time? If Ricky still had his real mom what would that be like? Would he go out on his own? Would she be sad if he did, or would she be happy? Or both at the same time? I wonder if anybody really thinks about that. What does the raccoon want out of life? How many of us animals and humans are on autopilot? And how many of us contemplate and take joy in everyday life?

Ricky left his enclosure and was out on his own for only a few days when I left the bedroom windows open for some fresh air. On a warm, late-summer night, I heard Ricky's familiar chirping as he called for me. He must have sniffed me out, as it sounded like he was outside the window. Since we were on the second floor, I thought it unlikely. The roof overhang was too far from the window for him to climb into. But he was on the roof in a panic, stuck like a cat in a tree. Ricky was pacing back and forth, chirping, not sure how to get down. Since I had kept him mostly away from the family, he didn't want to go to Howard. But I knew he was listening to me as I held the ladder, trying to convince him to come down. It was another Ricky-centric adventure, and I wasn't a fan of heights. I had to convince Howard, who was reluctant to climb the ladder, and persuade Ricky to climb on his shoulders. In the end, it took more begging to convince Howard to climb the ladder than it did to get Ricky to come down for some grapes. Ricky reached out for me, and I took him in my arms. Like a frightened child he wrapped his hands around my neck, and I carried him back to his enclosure where he spent the rest of the night, then slept all day. I thanked Howard with a hug and made him a special dinner that night.

I reluctantly opened the enclosure the next evening, and we had our little midnight trysts like nothing ever happened. He would run to greet me, swaying back and forth with joy as he trotted over. He would hug me, and I could feel his strength. But then he slowly drifted away, and I knew in my heart it would be okay. Although at times it was stressful and hysterically funny to raise him, I would miss it and him forever. I was glad to know him, and by being himself he made me feel that it was okay to be myself.

For a time after that night I couldn't sleep and would go out each night whispering for him. The third time was the charm, and he would come strolling out from nowhere rocking back and forth. His head held down, he would jump up on my leg or into my arms and give me a big, strong hug, and I would sigh, relieved that he still loved and remembered me.

After I planted the hot peppers in the garden, he stopped going there, except to eat the slugs and snails. I never heard one complaint in the neighborhood that there was a pesky raccoon around. This made me a proud, happy mama. After a time, when I went out at night to call Ricky, he stopped answering my calls. He was grown up and living his life, and I hoped it was a full one. I would have to find something else to do with my insomnia. It made my nights dull, and I felt lonely. We had a very special relationship. Those secret midnight rendezvous in my backyard and the time I spent with him was magical. I will never be able to repay him for the courage he gave me to accept myself as I am and to be a better parent. He will be forever in my heart and forever missed.

CHAPTER 12:

RESPECTING THE TOTEMS

As Ricky moved outside and away from my life, Coral Ann became a regular visitor. She was a very smart and charming salmon-crested cockatoo who put a love spell on anyone who met her. After work I came home to find her out of her enclosure, eating the wooden blinds and half of the molding around the window. I wasn't as charmed as I had been with her that morning.

She sat on the ledge of the sill. She took the piece of molding she was holding in her foot up to her beak and turned to me. She said, "What did *youuu*...do?" As if I had been the one who ate the window.

"Coral Ann...what did *youuu* do?" I said.

She responded by showing off her salmon-crested feathers, then bobbed her head up and down and laughed. And so did I.

There seemed to be a theme playing out in my life that I wasn't paying attention to. She was having a good time and didn't care what anyone thought of her. I thought I had gotten the message of self-acceptance and to loosen up from Ricky, but I could see I was sinking backward, and maybe Coral Ann was there to remind me.

As I was changing and growing in spiritual maturity, I knew I had glossed over something I hadn't felt ready to face.

Then, one day, I stumbled upon supporting evidence of what I needed to work on while browsing in a small bookstore. It was a book on animal totems. I read about how totem animals can have a significant spiritual meaning, acting as a spiritual guide by showing up in one's life offering messages for self-discovery by revealing our true nature with theirs.

Browsing through the book triggered a long-forgotten memory of the hawk I had seen on the beach while in Florida long ago. Howard and I had been married for less than two years when we went to see his sister in the Keys. Howard, me, his sister, and his brother-in-law were there with their baby and Melissa, who was a toddler then. We all went for a walk on the beach at the Gulf of Mexico and were planning on snorkeling. It was the first time I had seen the waters there. It was beautiful. My eyes were captivated by the calm, crystal-clear, blue-green water. My mind drifted from the conversation like a raft in the open ocean.

They kept walking and talking as I fell further behind.

I sat down in the sand and stared at the water, fixing my gaze on the horizon. I pulled my knees up to my chest and wrapped my arms around them. I noticed a speck of something moving in the sky, and it appeared to be making its way toward me. Even though I couldn't make it out, the bird held my attention. A hawk, I thought. When it arrived, it hovered over me, then landed on the sand next to me. It looked me in the eyes as if it knew me or was sizing me up. We sat there staring into each other's eyes. I felt as if it was waiting for me to say or do something, but there were no words.

Howard, with the family and Melissa, turned in surprise.

"Look at that!" my sister in-law exclaimed, pointing at the bird. "JoAnne, look up."

I smiled as she snapped a photo of me and the bird. It was extraordinary to sit with a bird of prey so close.

Then he flew off, leaving me in awe and wanting to know what the strange encounter was about. It stayed with me, and I often looked at the photo feeling like it meant something.

As I opened the book, I searched for the meaning of hawks. It said that encountering a hawk can mean that you should let your creative spirit flow. What a wild coincidence, as it was not long after that trip to Florida that I met the teacher who influenced me and helped me get into art school. There seemed to be something to this, so I bought the book.

When I got home, I was curious and looked up raccoons as totems. According to what I read, raccoons serve as a spirit animal that teaches us to be flexible and take the time to look at the big picture. A raccoon can symbolize letting go of a situation, person, belief, or habit and speaks to the importance of looking inward, to discover what could be blocking or delaying one's progress. Problem-solvers, raccoons represent a search for truth and solutions.

Ricky had taught me so much about how to be free with myself. But problems would always be near; however, my thoughts couldn't help but turn to an imbalance in my life *that was* weighing me down. A truth I didn't want to face.

It was my marriage and the way Howard treated me. My self-respect had been stripped away by an endless guilt trip imposed on me, along with constant criticism. For the whole of my life, it had been there. But the efforts I'd put in to be the wife Howard wanted weren't enough to keep him at home with us at night, and it stung deeply. Each year that went by, of what was to be fifteen together, felt as if I was sinking deeper into a pit of confusion about what Howard wanted. He flirted with and passed comments about other woman as if I wasn't there. It was humiliating, but I said little to him about it. I didn't know how to handle it as I had grown up in an environment where that kind of behavior was common.

Even though I worked I had gotten to the point that I felt I had to have his approval on any purchase other than food or paying for bills.

Since he was good at selling, and I had no confidence, I asked him to help me at art shows, justifying it with Howard that we would have a return on the investment. Howard once sold a car that wouldn't even start. I knew I was in trouble when I talked someone out of buying one of my paintings. He was persuasive and good at sales; I was not. Yet he never came to any of the art shows to help with sales, only to criticize me after. My hope was to be a team and assist him in achieving his dreams while he helped me with mine. Now I was fearful of what he would say when I wanted to send photos of my work to galleries.

Howard's friend stopped by one day, and I showed them slides of the new portfolio of my work that I had just put together.

Mike was a police officer that had told Howard about the school-crossing job and who I saw every day when I worked at the precinct. I had left that job not that long ago. Mike had a new baby, and for extra money he was moonlighting with Howard and me. It was a side business that we had going (from the gas station Howard owned) transporting trucks throughout the region. I got involved to bring in more money, organized the drivers, and drove the trucks myself sometimes, thinking it would also help our marriage to spend time together and grow Howard's business. Mike was authentic and never put on airs, like most of Howard's friends. Nor did he ever make a pass at me, like some of them. Howard was a jealous man with no reason to be so. Which was why I couldn't understand how he stayed friends with these kinds of men, even after I'd told him. They openly bragged about other women, but only when their wives weren't around. So, when Mike stopped by to pick up his pay, I was glad to see him. He was a real family man and had a sweet wife and was reliable. I gave him his pay first, then as I was showing him and Howard the portfolio, Howard interrupted and said with sarcasm, referring to my work, "Yeah, she's spending money on this stuff." As if it was a waste of money and time.

I felt a lump in my throat and my face getting red. I looked around to see if the girls had heard. Mike looked at me, then Howard, and said smiling, "It's an investment. How can she make money if she doesn't have anything to show? She's at least trying."

"It was only a little, it didn't cost much, and I'll make it up," I said looking at Howard. He knew me well enough to know how to feed my guilt until it opened like a raw sore. I felt so embarrassed. "But I've been selling some works," I said in defense of myself.

"Yeah," Howard scoffed, looking at Mike. "But can you pay the mortgage with it?"

"No." I wanted to run out of the room. I wanted to say that he spent so much money on himself at bars and God knows what else. But I just looked down and away. Anything not to make eye contact.

Mike sighed. "Why don't you give her a chance?"

I felt embarrassed and wished I'd never said anything. Had I been selfish wanting a career in the arts? Looking for a way to escape the conversation, I scanned the room and saw Melissa by the stairs, listening. Although I wanted to cry, I said nothing and did nothing.

Mike was defending me, and I was apologizing like a child. Something I found myself doing too often. I made an excuse that I had to get back to making dinner and said my goodbyes.

It was later when I was alone with Mellissa that she cut my heart by saying, "Why do you let him do that to you all the time? Why do you let him treat you that way?"

There was no answer to her question. Yet I could see from her eyes that any respect she had left for me had been lost. Even though she had spoken up to him in defense of me before. The memory of when I was a young teenager came flooding back. As much as I loved but at times feared my father, I had wished my mother would have left him. They were terrible together. I had asked her one day after my father had been gone for weeks and treated her so badly why she kept taking him back, why she stayed with him. She couldn't give me an answer, as I now couldn't give my daughter one. The whole thing made me feel like a victim. It's not that I wasn't one once, but that was when I was a helpless child.

I felt ashamed.

Was there a way to balance this life and make everyone happy?

Questions that led me to wishing I was someone else. But I was me, and my dreams and passions refused to go away, no matter how hard I tried. They would beg for attention, and letting go of them was like giving up the air that filled my lungs and kept me alive. So I held my breath and kept my head down, hoping for peace in my home as the tension built.

While Howard disappeared more and more and wanted very little to do with the care of our home, I began to do most of the home repairs myself. I was also teaching the girls what my father had taught me about cooking, home improvement, plumbing, and so on.

"Why do I need to learn how to hang a door, Mom?" Melissa asked, eyebrows together.

"Because you'll be able to fix anything yourself. You'll be self-sufficient."

As I drilled in the screws, she snapped back at me while holding the door in place.

"I'll just hire someone to do it!"

"Well, then no one can ever rip you off, as you'll know what to do and how long it should take."

I felt her thinking as she became silent, which was rare. Afterward I took the girls to the pet shop to get supplies. They had fun wandering around and playing with the birds and puppies. The owner, Marc, who got me the critter-sitting job, gave me steady work.

On some summer weekends, I would do a few art shows with my new work and was painting horses, my dog, and some other animals and landscapes. I wanted to prove Howard wrong about me. I also tried my hand at sculpting.

After going to see a talk from a wildlife artist I admired, who said he used plasticine sculptures to find the proper lighting for his painting, I decided to try it myself. That was the first time I realized I could see three dimensionally in my mind's eye, and sculpting came much easier to me them painting. I won best in show at a prestigious show in Manhattan with my very first sculpture, a bust of a leaping black horse, that I named *Leap of Faith*. It was what I was doing, taking a leap of faith and getting back to my art career—and bringing in a paycheck from it. I loved the medium of clay, but it was more expensive than painting. So I tried to do both whenever I could swing the extra cost after I sold a piece.

A local interior designer called me after seeing my work at a show and commissioned seven paintings. An art dealer I took my work to started buying from me, and I sold forty paintings that year. I was selling as fast as I was painting, mostly abstract landscapes and some animal paintings.

But it was never enough to prove my worth in my marriage. So, my big idea to prove Howard wrong about me no longer mattered, and I became self-destructive and was letting my art career slip away. There became this need to be accepted by Howard when I should have been kind to myself. But I wasn't, and maybe that was the problem. How could I expect someone else to respect me when I couldn't respect myself?

Then one night after a long day of working and picking up the girls from their after-school activities, I came home frazzled and exhausted.

"Okay," I declared to the girls, "start your homework, and I'll start dinner. Daddy will be home soon."

But I didn't have dinner on the table when he came home. I was making it, one of his favorites—London broil with homemade mashed potatoes, mushrooms, broccoli, gravy, and fresh out-of-the-oven bread. Through the years, I had taken pride in my cooking and learned how to speed, prep, and multitask efficiently in the kitchen. It always made me feel like I was back on the job I had once had as a short-order cook at the luncheonette during rush hour. I was also the host and waitress at that restaurant. I took those skills home with me. No matter how busy we all got I wanted my family to have a good home-cooked meal and tried to get us all to sit together. Melissa was helping me set the table when Howard walked in from work.

"Why isn't dinner ready?" was the first thing he said.

"Sorry," I said, looking at him for a hello as my stomach turned from not having dinner ready. "We got home late. It's almost ready."

He sat down at the head of the table, waited a few moments, then said, "I expect dinner to be ready when I come home."

It wasn't long after I was putting dinner on the plates as fast as I could. My mind was still rushing around my to-do list, so the words he said hadn't registered. While cutting up the meat for Julianne the words Howard he said next sunk into me like a heavy stone, carelessly thrown in a pond. It was when he spoke of our daughter in the third person: "Why can't she cut it herself? What's wrong with her? You should be serving *me* first."

Seeing my seven-year-old Julianne's confusion about what was going on and what she had done wrong, I looked back to my husband and saw him as a man I didn't know or want to. It made the apologetic woman I had become vanish. Always defending my position stopped in that moment, and I no longer cared about what he wanted.

I stood back from the table and took a breath. I looked at the girls, then told them to go upstairs and get ready to go, as we had to go out.

They went upstairs without a word. Then I called Baby over and gave her the dinner I had just cooked. She looked at me as if she'd won the food lottery.

Howard was in disbelief as he failed to understand. His eyebrows together, he appeared either confused or angry; I had no idea which, but I didn't care anymore.

With the full weight of my broken heart, I looked him in the eyes and said, "What I do for you is a gift. Because you were precious to me and *we* should be precious to you. I do this all because I love you. I don't have to do it, I want to. For you, for our family. Now you can make your own dinner."

Then I walked away. There was nothing more to say. It had gone on too long, and I couldn't bear to see that look in the girls' eyes. It was an anxiety and sadness I knew too well. I couldn't let them live in those emotions.

I called the girls down and said with the best enticement I could muster, "We're having pizza tonight. Let's go." And we walked out the door without looking behind us.

When I came home, Howard was gone for the night.

Then, on a Thursday night on a holiday weekend on our fifteenth wedding anniversary, I did what needed to be done. In the past, I smelled perfume on his shirts more than a few times and always knew the truth, but up until that night, and with the recent occurrence at dinner, I hadn't been ready to face it. Then that morning I found a number with no name in his things on our anniversary, and it gave me the strength I needed. So I sat alone in our living room waiting for him to come home. The girls had gone to stay with their cousins for the weekend. I started thinking about how many anniversaries and birthdays I had spent hours and hours planning for him and how many he had forgotten about me. It brought me back to my parents forgetting my sixteenth birthday. In school, all the kids had big parties, and I was forgotten by my own family. In a way I had been reliving that moment of feeling worthless and forgotten by the ones I loved. Then I remembered how many countless times Howard had told me he had no time for me or our girls, which brought tears to my eyes. But he always found time for his friends, playing pool, and car shows.

There I sat alone, feeling lonely, when he walked in the door. There were no flowers, no plans, no joy to see me. I didn't expect them anyway, as they were never really there. It was time, and I told him I didn't want to be married anymore and asked him to leave. He said he wanted to stay. But he didn't; I couldn't let him.

It was time to move on and face the truth. If I was to stay any longer it would be like standing on the bow of the *Titanic* as she sank, trying to scoop out the icy water with a bucket. We would have all drowned.

CHAPTER 13:
THE LOST-AND-FOUND DEPARTMENT

Except for some furniture and my favorite records, I had let it all go. The car and then the house that Howard wanted were all gone. I said, "Just give me full custody of the girls. We can split their expenses." Still, I was struggling to let go of the sense of loss and loneliness.

As persistent as rain in the rainforest, loss and loneliness had always found me.

My things in Brooklyn were gone but for a bag of clothing. Then everything but the clothes on my back at fifteen after we'd had a fire in the house. They were just things that could be replaced. It was the loss of people, my dogs, and pets that tore me apart. Especially when I thought of how some had died, such as in the fire. And here I was again starting over with the aftermath of the death of a relationship.

That emotional sting opened up a Pandora's box of past hurts and losses that for years I had painted over like I did with my art in college. And, like Humpy Dumpty, I had a great fall.

The evolution of my spirit required tears and falling apart. I had to let go of everything I had accumulated. I had to grieve for the sad little girl I once was, for my broken relationships. When our wedding song played on the radio, I cried for the broken promises and the band of gold I had given back. My mind wandered in conversations. I cried in the shower getting ready for the day and late at night trying to process my past and present. My career as an artist had suffered. Since the last few years, I had been working with Howard on his business. Now I was out of a job too.

Art had grown to be such a big part of my escape and expression, but my creative endeavors were pushed to the background as I struggled to survive, leaving me feeling as if the ground beneath my feet was as unsteady as I was.

To make ends meet, I worked two jobs, one as a cocktail waitress on the weekends at a high-end catering house in a castle, often working double shifts when the girls stayed with their father. That allowed me to be home some weekdays when the girls got back from school. But it still wasn't enough, so I worked doing animal-education programs at schools and animal birthday parties for kids at a pet shop.

The best part was that I was able to take the girls with me to work. They were always welcomed there and much loved by the staff. Julianne loved it and got to play with all the animals and talk to the customers. Melissa went to do the animal parties and photoshoots with me, and I was able to pay her as my assistant. It was a way of spending more time with them while trying to sort things out. My friends called me a fool for walking away with nothing. But I had the girls, and that was everything. My girls were the best part of me. They were the seedling in this world and needed nurturing.

But how, as a single mother, could I guide my teenage daughter into adulthood when I didn't learn how to from my mother and had struggled with it myself? Melissa was always my wild child and challenged everything I said. When I was a new mother, living in fear of everything, she was afraid of nothing.

It was all exhausting, and the running back and forth made it harder. Doing it in my crappy car made it almost unbearable. Driving to pick up animals, dropping off the kids, picking up the kids, dropping off animals, going back to work, and spending time with the girls. I was thirty-something and still had poor time-management skills. So, I was always late for everything.

My newly acquired ancient station wagon was so large, it was like driving a boat on land. We called it "the Beast." It had a big engine that made it known when you turned it on, and it ate gasoline like a starving crocodile in a river of goldfish.

I had run out of gas twice as the gas gage was broken. But it was still better than my first car as a single mother. The girls named that one "the Green Monster." It was puke green, rusted, and an eye sore. You could hear it croaking and grumbling and whining a mile away. Begging to be put out of its working life. It finally made its one-way trip to the scrapyard. It had to go after Julianne stepped to get in the back seat and put her foot through the floorboard. Howard was a mechanic and had found both cars for me. They were all I could afford at the time, but after the Beast, I decided I was going to pick out my next car.

Sunday came around again, and I had off work and was looking forward to spending the whole day with my girls. But Julianne had asked to go the beach, and Melissa wanted to go to her friend's house.

"Julianne, it's a weekend," I said. "It will be crowded. It's hot today, and you know how you can get overheated." Her wavy, blonde hair framed her face perfectly, and she was in full pout. She looked at me with her big brown eyes, blinking.

I sighed in defeat. "Okay, if you *really* want to go."

She grinned, bobbing her head like the bobblehead dog that used to sit on the dashboard of the car. But trying to get Melissa to go with us became futile, and I didn't want to push her and gave in to both girls' desirers for the day. While I understood that Melissa was a teenager who wanted to be with her friends, not her mom and baby sister, it was still disappointing.

Even though I had asked for it the wounds and the end of my marriage were still fresh. After our separation I still wasn't sure if Melissa loved or hated me for doing it. Julianne seemed more accepting and was happier than ever. But we were still struggling to find our routines as a family of three.

When I had dropped Melissa off at her friend's place, she got out of the car and said, "Bye, Mom, see you later." And for a split second, I could see my little sweet Melissa from when she was seven. It was something that brought me to tears remembering my little girl, even though her words now were dull, like an annoyed teenager. But not her eyes. I couldn't help but linger on the moment and the way the sunlight filled her face. I wasn't sure what it was, but it gave me hope. It made me think about how I missed the cuddles, hugs, and kisses when Melissa was a little girl. While driving to the beach I held close to a new idea that one day Melissa would come back around to me. I was sure of it. I just needed to be patient with her.

Over the years, I had enjoyed many peaceful walks on the beach with my feet deep in the cool sand during off-season, weekdays, and off hours watching seagulls pick at sand or hover in the air like kites held by an invisible string. It gave me time to think or to just be. When I was a lost, lonely teenager out on my own, the seashore mothered me, and the crashing waves lullabied me to sleep. The beach held my secrets, my hopes, and it was where I had planned my dreams. The girls and I flew kites, collected shells, and rode bikes on the boardwalk. Watching time wash away in small pleasant moments that became warm, loving memories. As I meditated alone, I became more aware that I was hypersensitive to the energy of crowds. The chatter and activity overpowered my senses, which was why I avoided going to the beach on the weekends in the summer and was stressing over it inside as we drove around looking for a parking space.

When I stepped out of the car the sound of the ocean's breathing was in my ears, its salty waters in my nostrils, and a faint taste in my mouth. While the experience was pleasant for the senses, it was too tiring for my arms after finding a parking spot so far from the sand. They labored holding a blanket, towels, a beach chair, and a cooler that was jam-packed with bottled water, juice boxes, snacks, and sandwiches. Holding Julianne's hand to keep her close on the crowded beach, I felt like a walrus with a pup, awkwardly walking to the sea.

Unpacking my beach bag, I pulled out my pacifiers, which included a sketchbook and pencils to draw, and a book to read. I had my favorite gray kneaded eraser to twist in my hands when I felt unsettled. We went to the water's edge with green plastic pails and shovels and started building a sandcastle. Julianne made friends with some children her age, and I was sent away with a mere gaze that said; *I'm good, Mom, you can go now.*

When I returned to the blanket, I took out my book to read but kept looking up every few words to see what she was doing. The kids had finished building, then happily destroyed the sandcastle. Not able to focus on my reading I gave up and grabbed my sketchbook. At first, I just doodled, then did some loose sketches of the children and seagulls. Drawing with my favorite eraser close at hand, getting ready to take back the lines I just drew, I fell into a trance. Some nameless thing came into my awareness. It was an energy I sensed but couldn't see. It had happened often. Generally, it had to do with animals. Because of it, I did well as a wildlife rehabilitator, animal trainer, and therapist because I connected with their subtle mood changes and energy levels. Though it didn't happen every time, it was enough to make me wonder how and why I was able to do this and others could not.

Looking for the source of that energy, I began searching. What my spirit had sensed was heading my way from the ocean. I lifted my sunglasses and squinted to get a better look. But in the sun's glare I couldn't determine what it was but continued to study it as it came to shore. And then, just as Mary from the sanctuary had said I would, I knew what it was. It was a common loon, and he was gliding across the water. The loon had gone from being an unrecognizable shape in the water, riding in the surf, to sand, and then finding his way to my side.

He stepped out of the water and, like my own child, found me through the crowd with ease and confidence. Confidence, something I was still lacking in its steadiness. It was constantly in the lost-and-found department.

The reason for the loon's presence at this beach escaped me, since I had never seen one before. He came up to me. I was more than mystified when he looked me in the eyes. It was as if I wasn't a stranger but a trusted friend. It's an odd feeling and hard to explain what it's like when a wild animal looks you in the eyes as if he knows you. His seemed relaxed. I couldn't help but recall the brief encounter when I was in my early twenties on the beach in the Florida Keys with the hawk. He had looked me in the eyes the same way.

I said hello to the loon who was standing to my right.

He answered with a shake of his feathers, then lifted one of his wings and groomed himself.

"Okay…," I replied, assessing the significance of his presence.

His grooming went on for a while as he meticulously went over every feather. When he stopped, he tilted his head to the sky, then back at me.

Mimicking him, I looked up too. I found imitating to be a good form of interspecies acknowledgment. Were we checking for hawks? None that I could see and said so. There were only small scattered clouds and the glaring sun and seagulls. Maybe he was checking the time by looking at the position of the sun?

I looked back at him and him at me. He looked healthy and a testament to plenty of fish in the sea.

Then he settled down, tucking himself as close to me as he could without sitting on my lap. So close that I could feel the faint brush of his feathers touching my bare thigh.

The loon was sleeping peacefully at my side when Julianne came trotting up for a juice box. She looked at the loon next to me as if it belonged there but still asked about it.

"What's that?" she mumbled as she sucked down the juice.

The loon didn't move. My daughter knew not to get too close to an animal she didn't know.

"A loon," I replied squinting and tilting my head to look up at her.

"Oh. Okay. I made some friends." She had moved on.

"I see—are you having fun?"

"Yeah." She nodded and smiled. "Are we keeping the loon? Did someone give it to you? Can I have another juice box and chips?" Her mind was like a jumping bean filled with questions. The sugar was surely kicking in.

I nodded, and she grabbed a second juice box and ran back to the water before I could answer any of her other questions.

Picking up my sketchbook and pencil I began sketching the sleeping loon.

Then people began to linger asking if that was my pet bird.

"No," I said, "it seems he just found me and decided to take a nap."

I kept my answers short and polite so they would move on and not wake my new friend. But almost everyone who walked by stopped to look and inquire. I had only half begun to sketch some vague outline of him, too distracted by the fact that he was here with me.

Then a familiar voice came from behind.

"Is that your loon?"

I turned my head. It was the pet-shop owner's partner.

"Oh, hi!" I was surprised to see him outside the shop and in a bathing suit.

"What are you doing here?" he asked looking around, then fixed his eyes on the loon.

"The loon just found me. He's taking a nap. Julianne wanted to come to the beach." My neck was hurting from twisting back and looking up as I didn't want to disturb my new friend.

"I thought you were bird sitting and took it to the beach." He laughed.

I giggled. "No, no," I said, as if the thought was ridiculous.

He only knew me from the pet shop and always saw me with some sort of critter. He also knew I took a lot of them home, mostly the ones that needed therapy. They called it training. I called it "critter therapy."

"All right," he said, looking toward the water. Beads of sweat dripped off him. He chuckled and shook his head. "I'll see you at the shop," he added and walked away.

I turned my attention back to the loon to see if we had disturbed him at all. His eyes were closed, head still tucked deep in his feathers in a peaceful slumber.

Leaning back in my beach chair I felt relaxed. I picked up my sketchbook and started to draw again but not with the intent to capture or study the loon in a physical form. My pencil lightly touched the paper, and like a hand flowing around on a Ouija board, I let it flow into a soft outline, a lasting impression of a soon-to-be memory.

The loon woke up an hour later and stretched his wings. Again, he looked me in the eyes and I slowly rose and stretched. I walked him to the shoreline and wished him a beautiful life as he made his way back to the sea. After a swim, and when Julianne was ready to go home, I got back into the Beast, my mood the opposite of when I'd arrived. Scatterbrained and stressed turned to a peaceful and meditative. It was as if I was with him in the serene ocean, floating along the current without any hurry to go anywhere or do anything. Food at my feet, sun on my back. What a peaceful existence as I enjoyed imagining what his life was like. Taking that feeling home with me, I slept like a baby.

Then one day the grieving was over, and the light of a meaningful future found me.

It was time to focus on a new beginning for me and the girls. At first it was hard as I processed my life, but I had nature to help me. Breakfast was no longer a battle with Melissa. We worked together, and if anyone said, "pass the sugar," we would all start sing the old *Sugar, Sugar* song from the sixties. We had monthly themes for dinner. The girls would pick a culture, I would go to the dollar store and buy stuff to fit the themes. We listened to music and talked and laughed more than we ever had. We would learn a new word or two and dance around. We were all learning something new and having fun doing it.

Since I had always taken life so seriously, fun was still a new experience for me. I was trying it on and then taking it back off for the coat of responsibilities. But I wondered if I could have them both. I also began to wonder if I could go back to school to get my BA, as I had been so close to finishing. So, I made an appointment and went into the city to see if I could get a loan or grant to finish, but I left the financial-aid department disappointed and couldn't fathom how I was ever able to go in the first place. I guess it was a strong will that had weakened over the years. It seemed not as important, and I was fine to hold off a bit longer—or maybe forever.

I had thought of the loon on the beach often after that day. He had helped me in so many ways. One was handling being around crowds. He did it so well, and I noticed how relaxed I was when I left the beach that day, because I was only focused on him and my daughter. That gave me a tool to work with, and I discovered new ways of tuning out all the noise in and out of my head. It helped to block out some of that overwhelming energy I found in large groups.

Curious after a long day I sat down to read about loons as totems. The book said that loons relied on water. Water, it said, was a symbol for dreams and many levels of consciousness, hence loons teaching us about following our dreams, hopes, and wishes for the future.

They're solitary birds with a voice that echoes a sad song of the wilderness on a lonely moonlit night. Was I destined to live now without romantic love? To sing a lonely song of want by the sea? Maybe I never really knew what love was. As it was hardly ever there to hold me and still my fears. Maybe my love and marriage were all smoke and mirrors of what I believed to be love. But could it be here in my new life? The loon showed me a different kind of love. A love and respect for oneself. A love and respect for myself was beginning to bud. It was a small bud. It found me as I entered the world of the wildlife and they entered mine. This wild world that I clawed my way into would surely be my forever love. The encounter with the loon had reminded me that alone is not *always* lonely. Summer would fly by as fast as the short days of winter felt long. And as it did my dreams turned pleasant, sometimes euphoric with dreams of wild horses, sleeping lions, and me flying just like a bird.

Chapter 14

Horse Lover Wanted

A hunger of change ran through me when I woke up that morning. There was a reawakening of the child in me, open to all possibilities. I imagined looking out the window and seeing horses in a field. Trees and singing birds surrounding us instead of parked cars and sidewalks. But also, an opportunity to give my girls the chance to discover their own dreams as I sought out mine. Inspired by nature.

After being a single mother for well over a year, the time had come to move from the neighborhood and memories of my failed marriage. The south shore of Long Island was beautiful; however, the house and neighborhood we lived in were what Howard wanted and what I had settled for.

So, after breakfast and the girls were in school, I gassed up the Beast and went out to chase a dream. It seemed crazy, but I trusted the instinct I had to find what my heart desired.

As I drove up to the north shore I couldn't help but think of how horses had become prevalent in my work and my dreams for the past six years. Drawing them in my journals. Dreaming, painting, and sculpting them. There was one dream that was so vivid it felt real. In it I stood with a paintbrush in my hand in front of a large blank canvas. Behind me was a field of horses of all different sizes and colors. A misty wall of nothing seemed to hold up the canvas. I swept my paintbrush back behind me and then forward onto the canvas. One by one the horses leapt on to the blank space. Some moved to the front while others faded into the background.

When I woke, I drew the dream, as I often did in the journal I kept at my bedside. Soon after I painted the dream horses on the largest canvas I had ever worked on. Some were loose and dreamy, others more realistic. The style of the painting was unlike anything I had ever done. It made me curious about the workings of the subconscious. The relationship of dreams and the power of intention.

After hours of driving on the curvy, tree-lined roads, my thoughts had shifted from art and houses and horses to hunger.

Seeing a chic strip of stores, I decided to stop to grab a bite. There were some boutique shops, a pizza place, and a farm stand. The farm stand had beautifully displayed flowers, fruits, and vegetables, and I could see myself shopping there one day. I bought a red apple, a bunch of flowers, and a couple local papers.

Then I went to the pizza shop next door.

Sitting down to eat my slice, I opened the paper to the classifieds. A part of me was feeling a bit defeated as I hadn't known what I was looking for but knew I hadn't found it yet. Regardless, I wasn't ready to give up. It was such a beautiful but wealthy part of the island. The wealth that was there wasn't what I was attracted to; it was the land, wildlife, better schools, and fresh start. The towns I drove through had big estates that didn't match my car or bank account. How could I afford to live there? The question loomed over me as I opened the paper and ate. I had hoped to find an answer to that question and why I felt so compelled to go on that day.

Then, there it was in black and white. The sign I had been searching for. My excitement boiling over like a whistling tea kettle when I read the words: "Horse lover wanted."

The ad was for an apartment over a barn on an estate with horses.

I sat reading the same three words over and over, not believing my eyes. Then I called the number to set up an appointment to see the place that day. I knew this was a rare opportunity that I wasn't going to let slip away. It was only ten minutes from where I was eating.

When I turned down a long gravel driveway and saw the old U-shaped carriage house, I giggled. There were goats in the barn and horses in the field. I didn't need to see inside to know it would be perfect. It was a hundred-year-old carriage house on a five-acre estate. A three-bedroom, two bath apartment above the stalls.

As I set out to greet the owner, in my excitement I forgot I was driving the Beast and had a moment of embarrassment, but the man in a T-shirt and jeans didn't seem to notice, or was it that he didn't care what kind of car I drove? We shook hands, and I was grinning like a child getting a double scoop of ice cream.

We went to the back of the barn and up the narrow staircase.

The kitchen was small, as I'd expected in such an old house, and had a small electric stove. I must have made a face or a sound I was unaware of because the owner who lived in the big yellow house said, "What is it?"

"Nothing." I stumbled over the small, lonely word. I wasn't sure if I should tell him the truth of my thought. But lying never suited me. He looked at me waiting for more. "Oh, it's nothing. I do love the place." I hesitated, looking around, then decided to trust my whole truth and share. "It's just that I love to cook, and the stove is so small."

"Oh," he said looking at the stove as if he had never seen it before.

"It's okay," I said." Turning away, I went back to look out the window at the horses. "I love the place. The horses are pretty. It would be wonderful to see them every day."

He sighed. "We mostly rent to college kids since the college is so close. But they move out in the middle of the night when they get behind on their rent."

"Well." I smiled. "I have two girls. We'll be sleeping at night."

He smiled back, and I followed him down the stairs.

"Okay, I'll be showing it to someone else in a few minutes."

I gave him my number. "Well, I would love it."

"It's two months' rent—in advance."

"That's fine. Thank you," I said.

As he followed me to my car, another car pulled in.

"I'll let you know and call you later today." He smiled waving to the next potential tenant as he walked away.

I knew in my heart it would be mine. I couldn't wait to tell the girls. But I did wait until it was finalized and I had the keys. He called later that day and said I could have it. But in my excitement, earlier that day I didn't ask what the rent was. And when I did it was too high for me to pay every month. I was honest about what I could afford and told him how I would make a great tenant. "I could clean the stalls and mow the grass, maybe barter for the difference? I'm also very handy," I said. When that didn't work, I tried logic. I said he had lost money, and it had taken more of his time to have the college students there at a higher price. With us he would be saving money in the long run. I was a single mother seeking stability in a home and would be there more than a few months. I would care for the place. My girls were good, well-mannered. He would never have to worry. He said he was sorry. I sighed, thanked him, and said my goodbyes. But I wasn't giving up. The next day, I found the address of the office of the paper where the ad came from and went there. The two gray-haired women in cotton dresses greeted me in the cramped, paper-filled office.

"I'd like to place an ad," I said. I brought the paper with me with the horse-lover ad circled in pencil. "I'm looking for this." I pointed at the ad.

They said something like this: "We know the owners; they often take ads out and have had trouble finding someone who can take care of the place."

"He told me," I said. "I wanted to rent it. I love it, it's just what I need." I gave a weak smile. They looked at each other, communicating without words.

"So, what's the trouble, young lady?" one said, but both smiled such a warmhearted, loving smile I felt as if I was conversing with friends or beloved aunts over a cup of tea.

"I'm separated—I have two girls, and I need a new home." I took a deep breath, for the next words that were coming out of me were so important, as they were my dreams said out loud and in public. It was as if the air leaving my body had invisible crystals of fireflies. It was coming out of the deep, dark forest to light up my words with its magic and wonder-filling fairy dreams. The words left my heart, and they were warm, pure, and clear. I felt as if I was floating, the way I did once in a dream. I continued to explain, holding back tears. I could see that they felt my truth, my passion for this dream home. "But…I was hoping he would come down on his asking price—it's just a little more than I can afford right now."

They looked at each other again, understanding. The other one spoke this time.

"This kind of rental here is very rare. It's a very wealthy community with very few rentals, never mind a horse farm."

"Oh," I said. I felt a pinch in my stomach. There were already too many coincidences, and now I was becoming an unwavering believer. Still believing in small miracles, I thought of the loon at the beach. Then only the previous day how on an impulse I found the horse farm. It was more than coincidences at play. If I had told anyone, if I had said it out loud, I knew it would have sounded a bit phooey-phooey. But I wouldn't be detoured or discouraged from believing.

After leaving the office and not placing an ad, I was perplexed but still believed it would somehow work out. I began to trust that by letting things go in my mind and not questioning that it would work out. So, I decided to spend a small amount of the money I had saved on a long weekend trip to let the universe work its magic and keep me from dwelling.

Julianne and I drove down to Charleston, North Carolina, on Valentine's Day weekend. There was a wildlife art festival that I loved going to, and so did the girls. It was a new tradition for us. But when I took them both, they fought all the way down and seemed to compete for my attention. So, we all agreed that I would take one and switch every year. They then could get my full attention. No sibling rivalry. Mellissa stayed with her father. Julianne was excited; she had taken the separation better than my eldest. They both accused me of playing favorites, which made me laugh. They didn't know how strongly I felt about the subject. My mother had always shown that she had favorites, and I was always last on the list of the four children. I swore I would never be that way with my children, and I wasn't. As each one said the other was my favorite, I would say, "You know your sister says the same thing about you."

But they never got what I was trying to say, no matter how many ways I said it. It was when I spent the time alone with them that I could see them shine and found that it helped in the balance of our relationship.

While sitting in traffic on a narrow road after crossing into South Carolina, Julianne asked me a question as she stared out the window, deep in thought. "Are we lost?"

The way she said it made me think. Was she asking where we were in the world or where we were in our lives? It seemed more likely to be the latter, so I assured her with confidence, "Mommy knows where she's going." In that moment I wanted to tell her about the horse farm, but I wouldn't until I could find us a new home.

We did a little shopping, and I brought two stone pedestals to take home with us, and Julianne got some trinkets to remember the trip by. We ate fried green tomatoes, and I thought of my father and that he would have liked the way they made them. He also would have loved the horse farm.

We took in the sights and went for long walks on the old cobble-stone streets. We saw wildlife and wildlife art from some of the best contemporary artists in the world. I bought autograph books from some of the artists and talked to them as if I was a groupie backstage at a concert. Normally, I would sweat every purchase. Since I grew up poor and was out on my own so young, I knew what it was like to go hungry. But I had grown a new faith in myself and our future. Before I was always waiting for the next drama ball to drop. It was something I was trying hard to let go of. I was working to be a better me. As we drove home, I thought only of the memories I would cherish forever. I wasn't going to worry about anything else.

A message was waiting for me on my home answering machine when I returned. It was the man from the horse farm. "I don't know what you said to the ladies that own the paper, but they scolded me and said I would be a fool not to let you have the place." He paused, then added, "And the rent will be what you asked. Call me back and let me know. Bye now."

That message was two days old, and it was a quarter after nine and felt like it was too late to call. But I did anyway.

"Hi," I said. "It's JoAnne with the girls. We came to look at the place last week. I know it's late, and I'm sorry, I was away. I usually don't call anyone after nine, but I wanted to call you and let you know I got your message and thank you. I would love to have the house. I can call you tomorrow, if you like, or I could just come over."

"That will be fine. I'll be home, say, around three?"

"Great, and thank you again." I was smiling from ear to ear.

"I'll see you tomorrow."

I jumped up and down and swung my head and arms around like a crazy person. The next day, after I gave the landlord the deposit and got the key, I went home and sat the girls down. "Do you like horses?" I said with a giggle. They looked at each other and me with curious faces. Because they knew I already knew the answer, and it was a hard yes. "We're going to live on a horse farm!" I declared with waving arms.

I drove them over to see the place. They were as excited as I was, and after all the sadness we'd been through, I was thrilled to see them happy. I knew we would find the peace and love in our little family together, sleeping under the stars and above the horses.

The day we moved in the landlord surprised me with a brand-new, full-size stove.

He walked me into the kitchen pointing to the new stove. "So you can cook whatever you want for your girls, even a Thanksgiving tur-key," he said with a bashful smile.

It was overwhelmingly thoughtful, and I told him how grateful I was. I made an apple pie and brought it to the big yellow house. They invited me in for tea and said if I had to work late the girls were welcome to come over and, in the summer, go for a swim in the pool.

They had two children who were close to Julianne's age.

It didn't take long after we moved to made friends and barter with one of the horse borders. She was a horse vet who owned two horses that lived in the barn. I learned how to muck the stalls and occasionally turned them out and fed the horses, goats, and barn cats.

Sometimes the girls would help. Then I learned how to ride with JoJo, a dark-brown retired racehorse. He had a strong white band going down the front of his head. He was a good size and had large, brown, expressive eyes that often looked worried. He was afraid of rabbits and paint cans, and jumping frogs made him rear up.

JoJo, who I fell in love with at first sight, took a little longer to reciprocate his love for me as he had been moved around to a lot of barns and different people. But I quickly grew on him as I learned to ride. He taught me so much about horses. I rode, groomed, and played with JoJo, and the girls would get on him for a slow walk around the property.

The small art studio that was once an empty barn stall drew JoJo's attention. Looking around and moving very carefully, he smelled the clay, the canvas, and the brushes. I found out later that it was once his stall. We would chase each other in the field. I'd run toward him calling out, "I'm going to get you!" He'd rear up whinnying, and shake his head, then run off with me chasing him. He would let me catch him, then I'd run away, and he would catch me, then hang his head over my shoulder. I'd rub his nose, kiss him, and tell him how much I loved him.

We watched the sunsets together with the girls. We got a puppy. A cocker spaniel named Stella, Italian for star, because she had a little white one on the top of her head. Stella went everywhere with me and slept under the covers, like a person.

I woke up in the morning to Stella's rust-colored, fury face on the pillow next to me.

She would have the covers up to her shoulders looking like a tucked-in child. She ate my sandwich, sat in my chair at the dining room table. Stella was in the barn with me, in the car with me. Almost everywhere I was, she was. Like Julianne and sometimes Melissa, Stella went to work with me. I had gotten her at the same time that the landlord had found an abandoned kitten. Niles lived in the barn with the other three cats and had a fascination with Stella, who was around the same age. Niles would wait for us on the other side of the barn door and jump out to surprise us, which was no surprise since he did it every day. He would jump up, pretending to box Stella's face. Stella would just raise her paw in a handshake. I did a small sculpture of the two of them in that pose. When I did the chores Stella would eat everything except her own food.

Melissa threw me a birthday party that year, and Julianne was trying to find me a date. She was still too young to leave alone, and Melissa was too old to want to babysit. They were seven years apart. So, Julianne went to hang out at the pet shop after school while I worked. She had fun, and everyone knew and loved her. She knew so much about animals and loved to talk to the customers and some of the bird breeders. She picked a man for me who bread parakeets and had a son her age. Julianne introduced me as her single mom and winked at me from behind him.

He walked me to the car and said, laughing, that my daughter said we should go out.

I laughed, then he said, "Would you like to go out to dinner, maybe?"

"Oh, thank you, but I can't right now." I could hardly finish my sentence, and now we were both embarrassed.

After he left, I called Julianne over, and we sat in the car.

"Julianne, what were you thinking?"

"Mom, it's time; I don't want you to be alone."

"Honey, I'm not alone. I've got you and your sister."

She twisted her mouth and said, "I know, but it's not the same. He's nice. He likes animals and has a kid too."

"Do you like his son?" I asked.

She nodded. She did like him.

"Well, I do appreciate it, and he seemed nice, but I'd like to do it when I'm ready, okay?"

She nodded again and said, "Okay, Mom. I love you."

"I love you too."

As we settled in and summer came around, I found life was perfectly delicious. The life I had once lived had left my mind like a bad dream. I painted without guilt that I should be doing something more important with my time and began sculpting regularly. I was also teaching and learning how to love and trust people as much as I trusted animals. My new work included school programs about animals, talking to Boy Scouts and Girl Scouts, sick and disabled children, and going to nursing homes and watching people light up.

I never felt more alive and purposeful.

When I pulled the car in at home in the afternoons, JoJo would run to the end of the gate. I was excited to see him and made it a point to give him my undivided attention. He wasn't mine on paper, yet we were bonded by our hearts. When I couldn't sleep, I would go down to the barn and check on the horses and stare up at the stars. It would often make me think of my sweet Ricky the Racoon and our midnight meeting in the yard. Sometimes I'd find my way to the studio and work. Most times, however, I'd find myself by JoJo's side.

JoJo was laying down when I came to see him in his stall one night. It must have been three in the morning. The moonlight entered with me as I opened the creaky door. JoJo barely lifted his head, and his eyes spoke in the shadow on the full moon: *Oh, it's you.* His eyes were soft and sleepy. I wondered what it would be like to lay next to him. I had seen this in movies, and it seemed so peaceful and serene, such a bond between human and horse. I wanted to know this moment for myself. I thought JoJo would get up, but he didn't. He laid his head back down. I dropped to my knees and put my head on his massive chest and reached up to stroke his neck. He let out a huff of air, and I could hear his heart breathing life into his body. I took a deep breath, and for a moment I felt outside myself looking in at this tender moment of true love.

My spirits renewed, I thought about the sanctuary and how Mary had introduced me to wildlife and helped me get my rehabilitator's license. She trusted me to raise Ricky, who gave me a better understanding of myself. I was done painting horses for the moment and wanted to paint more wildlife.

It had been a while since I had gone to the sanctuary. This time I went with a different purpose than volunteering to clean the aviaries and feed the birds. I wanted to talk to Mary about having a wildlife art show there. Living closer to the sanctuary it would be easier to get more involved. The art show could be part of a fundraiser for them. Mary liked the idea and said I should come by again to talk over the details. She was in her office when I said goodbye. The blue jay who had grown up in that office was circling the building as I left. I knew it was him when he said hello and called out like a red-tailed hawk. After a short walk on the trail and a visit to the hawks, owls, and falcons, I left.

The next afternoon, when at work picking up animals from the pet shop, things were going so well I had put aside my fear of waiting for the ball to drop bad news in my lap. In this unguarded state, I was unprepared for the news I was about to hear.

"Did you hear about Mary?" Marc, the pet-shop owner, asked.

"What?" I said, moving around the counter to hear him better. "I just saw her yesterday."

"She's dead. She was in a car accident."

I felt myself sweating and shaking and looked him in the eyes. "But I just saw her." I was sick and confused. "I have to go. I'll call you later about tomorrow's work." I rushed out.

The news had set me off, and I felt the darkness of my past seeping in. The unstable life of tragedies and unexpected deaths of people who were too young to die. Because I didn't know how to deal with the emotions, I didn't. I just shut down.

Her family and personal life were unknown to me. We never got together outside of work; our relationship was all about the love of animals and nature. Yet I felt the pain and sadness of loss that I seemingly had no right to feel. I called the sanctuary and said how sorry I was, but I couldn't go back there. There would be sadness, and I felt lost about what to say. What if I said the wrong thing? Death scared me, and I was yet to understand why.

As my heart continued to heal from other recent wounds, I couldn't linger on that question of why or take on any more sorrow. As the evolution and healing of one's heart takes time, the examination would have to wait for another day.

CHAPTER 15:
HORSE'N AROUND WITH CELEBRITIES

As I drove down the curving roads of Westport, Connecticut, I felt as if I was driving to a secluded home, not a television studio. Passing the large houses in lush country settings, I wondered what kinds of wildlife lived there. And how they fared among the well-groomed gardens, stone walls, gates, fences, and manicured lawns.

When I arrived, I looked down at the printed directions to make sure I was in the right place. But nothing about it felt right, for I was out of my comfort zone. I reluctantly pushed the button on the box next to the gate. "Hello," I called out, then sat there waiting for someone to answer. Soon I heard a crackle from the little speaker. "Hi, I'm the animal handler," I said. "I'm here with the canaries from the pet shop." The gate opened.

For the last few years I had worked mostly on local cable television and some morning talk shows in Manhattan. It was great being on sets, but it was something I had never imagined I'd be doing and still felt a little out of my depth. In the process of heading down the driveway and parking the car, I'd considered the reasons for my apprehension.

Was this uncomfortable feeling a result of assuming I wouldn't have anything in common with anyone here? Or was it that I felt like I'd be judged for my cheap shoes, jeans, and the Brooklyn accent that I'd tried to eradicate? But it stubbornly hung on. More than likely it was my insecurities and I was judging myself. I concluded I didn't know a lot about the shows I had worked on. Nor did I know much of the backgrounds and lives of the celebrities who hosted or appeared on them. Some of them I briefly met over muffins, fruit, and beverages in green rooms.

Then, there were the television appearances that added to my insecurities of not belonging in the world of live TV. One faux pas was when I went on the *Montel Williams Show* with Shelby, a small monkey I worked with and cared for. The show was a about a hypnotist who made Montel's guests believe they could talk to animals, among other things. Before the show I was shown where I was to sit. It was next to two big rottweilers. After seeing the dogs, I knew Shelby wouldn't like being so close to them. Shelby liked dogs but had to get to know them in an environment she was familiar with.

Turning to the stagehand, I said, "Oh, I don't think Shelby would like that." Meaning being so close to two big dogs. As I'm naturally soft-spoken I have been often asked to repeat myself. I wasn't sure he heard me because he walked away. Before I could say anything else it was showtime. One by one, Montel introduced each guest. The dogs followed their handler out. Then it was my turn.

Montel introduced me, and I walked on stage with Shelby in front of a live applauding audience. Shelby had pulled my hair. She did that when she wanted something or was anxious. She had done this so many times before that I went on autopilot and forgot we were live with *a lot of people* watching. Wanting us all to have a good time, and seeing the empty chair at the end of the stage and away from the dogs, I trotted over with Shelby and sat down. This was not what I was supposed to do. It was Montel Williams's chair! Boy did Montel look surprised. While Shelby was content, Mr. Williams's eyes got wide, and I gulped when I realized what I had done. I gave him my best *sorry* eyes. He moved on with the show like it was planned.

After the segment Mr. Williams walked over to me. "You know you sat in my chair," he said with a chuckle.

"I'm sorry, but Shelby was scared of the big dogs," I said as I pointed to where the dogs had been.

He shook his head and seemed to be understand. He had very kind eyes.

I continued to explain. "An upset monkey on live TV—" But before I could finish, I was ushered away by a stagehand as they were at the end of the commercial break, which was good because I didn't even know what I was going to say next. Montel gave us a small wave.

It wasn't the only time I forgot it was live TV. Like one early morning on a news show, not my best time of day. As the animal handler my job was to hand off one of the birds to whoever was the expert on the show, then slip away out of view of the cameras but close enough to take the animals when queued. That day it was a sulphur-crested cockatoo that flew off. Although most of the birds could fly and did so on sets more than once, it would take a little sweet talking to get them back down. In these moments I became focused on the animals, and everything else disappeared. But that day the bird flew off right in the middle of a live segment. He headed toward the cameraman, and I went after him. People at home, I heard later, saw my unpowdered nose getting closer and closer, until my nose filled the lens! I felt embarrassed, self-conscious, horrified. Wondering if I had any blackheads and if I did how they had been seen in people's homes!

In a strange way, remembering those uncomfortable moments as I put the car in park at the studio calmed me and allowed me to laugh at myself.

"We're here," I announced to the canaries as I took them out of my SUV. After a deep resetting breath, I lowered my shoulders and entered the Martha Stewart Studios more poised.

It was quiet and took a few minutes before I found someone who guided me to the set.

"Hi," I said to the blonde woman with the headset on. "I'm Jo-Anne, with the canaries." I smiled and held up the birdcage as a point of reference. "I think Martha's expecting me. Do you know where we're supposed to go?"

Martha Stewart had entered my life by way of cooking and entertaining books that Melissa had collected. Melissa loved entertaining as much as me, and I enjoyed decorating. Martha's magazine had helped with some gardening tips. We watched her show when we could, but it was on at a time when I was usually working. Otherwise, I knew little except that she was a very clever, successful businesswoman and well organized, as I saw at the television studio that day. There was something to be learned from a woman like that.

The seven yellow and orange canaries tweeted as we walked down the hallway to their new home. It was a large, wood-framed, homemade enclosure, painted gray with hardware cloth and a multitude of large and small doors. It was in a room that was created to looked like a room in someone's house. Mirroring Martha's house, I imagined; however, this room, or any of the rooms in the studio, didn't have any normal ceilings, just a maze of lights.

After I made sure they had food and water, I one by one took them out.

"Okay, babies," I whispered after all of them were in the enclosure. "You'll be happy and well taken care of." As Martha would be bringing them to her home.

A studio hand with a headset told me to stick around and "feel free to get breakfast." She gave me directions to the kitchen/cafeteria that smelled like a Sunday-roast dinner. While making tea I heard a voice behind me. There were two other people in the room. A woman with short blonde hair with her back to me talking to a man who was facing me. After a quick glance over, I returned to my tea.

Thinking how sweet of this woman to caringly show a man how to make a perfect cup of cappuccino. He was dressed in work clothes, as if he had been working outside—perhaps the gardener? He listened, politely watching what she was doing.

I didn't know who he or the woman was, only that her voice sounded familiar. It wasn't until I walked out of the kitchen and was halfway down the hall that I realized it was Martha Stewart. It was so unexpected to see her there, and it made me chuckle. Because in my imagination she would be sitting in a glamorous dressing room filled with flowers and fresh fruit, wheeling and dealing a muted pastel palette for her new line of whatever.

While wandering back I peaked in to beautifully decorated rooms with fresh flowers—rooms I'd love to have lived in. I had always appreciated Martha's sense of style. Her rooms and color palette had a peacefulness to them—something I'd strived for in my own work and home.

When I returned to the room with the birds they were chatting away and looked like they were enjoying the space. Their excitement became mine, for I loved when animals were happy. I was so lost in the world of canaries I became startled when the dimly lit room suddenly exploded with bright light.

A flow of headset people adjusting knobs on handsets entered. I felt like I shouldn't be there and looked around for a place to hide.

"She's walking," someone said, and everyone moved around like soldiers on a mission. I wondered if they were getting the sets ready to film. As I looked for a place to go a woman with a headset came over and ushered me behind a fake wall on the other side of where the birds were. She talked and gestured me were to go. I felt foolish, like a new faux pas was coming my way. "Stay here, and be quiet," she said as her eyes scanned the room. I tucked myself further back behind the set wondering if I'd be in trouble for bringing my tea to the set. Not wanting to be caught with the evidence I looked around for a garbage can as I sucked down the rest of the hot tea. But there was none to be found, and I burned my throat and was now left holding an empty cup. While I waited and listened for the queen of perfection to walk in, I thought of my first celebrity encounter. It was when I got to work with my childhood hero Jim Fowler, a wildlife expert of Mutual of Omaha's *Wild Kingdom*. It was such a thrill. He was exactly the same person in the green room as on the set and in my imagination. Jim treated me like a long-lost friend, as he did with everyone he met. Over the last few years Jim had touched my heart with his love, passion, and generosity giving his time to anyone who asked a question about animals. He loved animals and talking to people about them as much as I did, and that was the common ground we connected on. I became a regular handler for Jim on the *Today Show* and other talk shows, then later helped him with a show he had produced about prairie dogs.

We did the *Conan O'Brien Show* together, which was one I had been familiar with since it was on at night—my favorite time of day. Conan was as funny and nice backstage as on the show, and it was delight to meet him.

Soon Martha came into the room and sounded pleased to have the birds there and started talking to them. As I lingered and listened, I began contemplating if I would get to meet Martha Stewart and if she was nice, or if I would have to hide behind the wall until she left. Then I heard her say, "Where's the bird wrangler?"

The woman who had told me to stay and be quiet came over to get me. I put the empty cup down and stepped out. Being an introvert, it was a challenge not to want to run away, as I became aware that everyone was looking at me.

"Hi, I'm JoAnne," I said, looking at Martha while walking to the birds for moral support. "I brought the birds. I love the enclosure; they'll be happy here."

Martha responded. "I designed it myself."

It was inspiring, and I was a little surprised, as it was a thoughtful design for the birds.

"Really? That's amazing. It's perfect for them."

She then summoned her assistant and told her to send me the plans for the aviary at no charge. I thanked her, and a bridge was crossed for the love of animals. There was very little separation, and it no longer mattered where I came from and how I spoke, we both loved the sweet songs of a canary.

Later, when I went home, the girls were so excited to say that the *Martha Stewart Show* had called the house and they wanted to know if I'd met her. "Yes," I said. They looked impressed. It was easy to impress the girls when they were little. All I needed to do was make them a cake or cookies or homemade macaroni and cheese or fresh bread or bring home animals or tell them a funny story. When they turned to a two-digit age it became much harder to do. Recalling the first time we took Melissa shopping at the mall when she was twelve. She turned to me and said, "Can you walk behind me so my friends don't see you with me?" I was crushed. Yet here I was back to being a cool mom. Standing tall, I said "Yeah, I'll be working there, and look, Martha gave me plans for a canary enclosure." They looked at it and asked if I was going to build it. "Maybe, but it's a bit big for here."

After that I worked on her show when there were animal segments, then another show she produced on keeping pets. As her seven canaries became twenty-two, Martha gave a few canaries away to the staff, and I took one. Petey had deep-yellow feathers with orange undertones that reminded me of a sunflower. It was such a wonderful gift. Never having a canary as a pet before I didn't realize how delightful it was to wake up to. In my opinion, the variety and complexity of his songs were the best of any canary who has ever sung. Petey sang in the mornings and when particular songs would come on the radio, like "Hocus Pocus" by Focus or David Ruffin's "My Whole World Ended" and old Motown songs. Petey especially liked the Temptations. Whenever he sang, he puffed out his chest with the pride of a silverback gorilla.

He also enjoyed some classical music, but I can't remember what. Nevertheless, like Julianne he would never sing along to a country song. The confidence Petey had in himself was contagious, and it grew in my new job and in the world of television and influenced my art career. This Shangri-la, I thought, somehow would last forever.

Then one spring morning I saw a peregrine falcon sitting on the horse fence outside the big bay window in front of the house. It was as if the falcon was waiting for me. I stepped outside, and he didn't fly away.

I felt a twinge of nerves in my stomach. Strange.

It was odd because I had connected to the peregrine falcon as a warrior, as a symbol of freedom. But not that day. He finally flew away, over the barn and over my head, and as he did, it was if he was warning me of what was to come. There were new hard life lesson to learn, and I would need all my inner warrior, strength, and, to my surprise, a small bird to help me through it.

CHAPTER 16:

MY BROKEN WING

The smell of hay, pine trees, and honeysuckle had become a familiar scent to me during my six years on the estate. A perfume of bliss that I knew I would never forget. Life had a flow to it. We had house parties and went to dinner with new friends. It was far from a chore to muck the stalls or exercise and groom the horses. Our summer garden was full of white and purple pansies and violet impatiens in terra-cotta pots. My company as I worked in the garden and art studio was an eclectic mix of furry and feathered friends. There was my cocker spaniel, Stella, Henry the peacock, two goats, four barn cats, and a large white rabbit named Sam. The neigh and nicker of horses became routine as afternoon tea.

At the nearing of forty, I found myself in a distinct place in my being, and I greeted it with open arms. The freelance work I did on sets and photoshoots were as exciting as the new people I met. I was entering prestigious art exhibitions and winning ribbons and recognition for my work. Melissa was twenty and had moved out to create her own life. Julianne would be going into high school, and faraway adventures were calling to me.

First on the list was Africa. Home to lions, elephants, rhinos, giraffes, and zebras. The brochure I had for a tented safari in Kenya had become worn and dog-eared from turning the pages and staring at the photos with longing and excitement, dreaming of what it would be like. Maybe I'd volunteer my time and some of my art for an international conservation organization. Perhaps help with wildlife research in exotic places or possibly go on an artist retreat. Yet once I started saving for that long-lost dream of a trip, a fear and realization began to rise. As much as I recognized how much I had evolved, I could see there were things that still lurked in the darkness of my subconscious. I could feel them clinging to the edges. It dawned on me that for most of my life, I had viewed happiness with suspicion. Was it from having so many disappointments? Like being so close but not achieving my bachelor's degree? Or was I afraid to experience world travels and wildlife adventures, following in the footsteps of my childhood hero, Jim Fowler, and others who I'd admired?

So many desires were given up for more practical things.

Sometimes it made me feel like George Bailey in *It's a Wonderful Life*. Bags packed and ready to go, but my person or money was required elsewhere. A punch in the stomach of a dream that may never be realized. Yet I did have a wonderful life, and if I had a magic wand to go back in time there would be very little I would change. Still the fear lingered as I got closer to realizing my dreams of world travel.

And then it came. The punch that took away more than the dream of an Africa safari. I had turned forty in the fall with great plans for the coming years. By spring, out of nowhere, a pain in my right side grew to a doctor visit. The diagnosis was a diseased gallbladder and an obstruction in the bile duct caused by a large stone. The doctor I was referred to had prestigious degrees on his wall and seemed like a nice guy who promised I was in good hands. He said that I needed to have my gallbladder and stone removed. I was assured it was a simple operation and that I'd be fine. I would be home in a day and back at work within a week.

But it wasn't fine. The day after the operation the doctor came to see me in my hospital room. I told him I didn't feel well and was having a lot of pain. His manner had changed from the nice man I had met in the office. He was short and annoyed at my complaints when he examined me. He wouldn't look me in the eye and seemed in a hurry to leave. He said he had a hard time, and the operation took longer than it should have but insisted I go home. He said he was sending me home twenty-four hours after the operation, as planned. I pleaded with him.

"I have a very high tolerance for pain, but it feels like something is really wrong."

"Everyone goes home today," he said, then added something about the insurance company not liking the doctors to keep the patients. Was he saying that pleasing the insurance company was the priority, or did he just not believe me?

He ignored me and walked out of the room. I had remembered reading that Andy Warhol had died from complications following a surgery to remove his gallbladder. A wave of panic filled me. I wished I had never had the operation. As I rang the hospital nurse, I became afraid and angry at myself for not getting a second opinion. When the nurse came in, I told her how I felt and what the doctor had said. I asked if anyone was able to help. No, she said, that was up to the doctor, and he said I was being discharged.

It felt like someone was ripping my insides out as I struggled to the car, then to my bed. Alone with Julianne, I laid there helpless. As the light faded from my bedroom window and night fell the pain had become unbearable and my voice weakened. I called out to Julianne for help in faded whispers. Over and over trying to carry my voice across the house.

It felt like one of my nightmares of when I was a child. In the dreams the terrors were so great that my voice went silent. My inner terror welled up as I realized no one would save me, and I couldn't save myself.

Julianne finally came in the room. I wasn't sure if she had heard my calls or was just checking on me. Either way it was a relief to have her there.

"Help me. Call the doctor," I said.

She did and told him I was in a lot of pain, but again my doctor didn't listen and told her I must have gas and should take some Tums and rest. Hot tears trickled down my face. I felt I was dying. Disappearing in and out of consciousness, I lost all hope for any kind of help.

Later that night, my older sister came over. She called the doctor and told him I said I felt like I was dying. The doctor told her I was fine and should just take Tums. My sister hung up and called an ambulance. Then she called the doctor back. When she told him she had to call an ambulance, she said that all he said was "Oh my god" and hung up on her.

Every moment became unbearable as they carried me from my bed into the ambulance. We passed Julianne on the way out. She was holding Stella, and they looked worried. Seeing Julianne so frightened made me worry that she would be traumatized from seeing her mother taken away. She needed me, and I was helpless to comfort her.

The agonizing ambulance ride to the closest hospital was in vain, as they wouldn't treat me. I never knew why. They just put me back in an ambulance and sent me down to the hospital that had sent me home. It felt like I was being burned alive from the inside.

Where my own doctor was, I didn't know. I went into emergency surgery wanting to scream, but no sound came out. I remember choking on the mouthpiece and felt the tube going down my throat as they started an IV. No one told me what was happening. There were no words of comfort.

Then the blackness finally came. It was a relief to know I would soon be unconscious. There was a humming in my ears as I fell into a dark tunnel.

I had a severe bile leakage that had turned to sepsis. I found out later that the bile leakage I had wasn't drained properly, which left me internally scarred and the bile duct and liver permanently damaged offering me a new life with chronic pain.

Several months after the emergency surgery, sitting across the large desk from the doctor who did that surgery, my hands felt shaky, my nerves on edge as I listened to what he had to say about my prognosis. He leaned forwarded and put his elbows on the desk and folded his hands in front of him. It was then that he said that what had happened to me would severely shorten my life. I didn't say a word. I didn't ask any questions. I just nodded, and when he was done, I thanked him for his time. I left his office and sat in the car—for how long, I can't remember. My body felt cold, and I started to shiver. I turned the radio up as loud as it could go to drown out the feelings of despair. As I watched the cars and people go by and disappear down the four-lane road I wondered who they were and what their life was about. Were they happy? Did they live their dreams? But as I tried to distract myself a thought kept creeping back. It was supposed to be an easy surgery, and now I would regret it for the rest of my life. Regret was something I promised myself I would never have. But there I was sitting with regret and embracing it like a long-lost friend.

After that I was in a tailspin of hospitals, doctor visits, procedures, and told I would be on medication for the rest of my life.

Months, then years went by as I sat alone across from one doctor after another having so many tests and procedures as my health continued to decline. I was offered long-term pain medication but refused it, taking only what I needed to get me through the first few days after a procedure. What I didn't want was to go through life addicted to drugs or live in a brain fog. Instead, I had biofeedback to help manage my endless pain.

I had pancreatitis at least four times, and each time it took months to heal. I then had to have the sphincter in my pancreas removed since it was so badly scarred.

Once again, I would go into the hospital for another procedure.

The day before that procedure I wanted to be in the garden. I knew that I might not survive, as the doctor had told me the mortality rate was high for these kinds of procedures. If I did survive it wound be another long hall of healing, and if I didn't have the procedure, it was only a matter of time, as the bile duct was blocked again, and my liver was in distress. It was something I couldn't put off any longer, and if I was to die, I wanted to spend my time with my family, then some time alone, close to the earth to feel the dirt in my hands and the beauty of nature in my heart.

It didn't take long before I had to sit on the heels of my feet to relieve my back and nausea. As I sat kneeled in the garden, it wasn't lost on me that the way my body was posed was reminiscent of my church days, kneeling on the hard, well-oiled, pine-smelling benches in prayer. My mind kept going back to the days I had prayed in that church and the old days of morning mass. I often felt like I was the only one praying.

Since I left Brooklyn, my church was in nature, the ground as my bench; my faith was in the soil and my deep connection with the earth and all the beauty it held. If I trusted that there was a bigger plan, and if it was my time to go, I was scared but accepting.

As I leaned back from the small garden in the afternoon sun against the old carriage house, I took it all in. My anger for what had happened faded to sorrow.

When I looked out to the fields my heart reached out for JoJo. I wanted to be with him, but it was too far for me to walk without being out of breath, so I turned back to the garden.

The soil, sun, and my love for the earth had turned into a jungle of vegetables.

While the horses in the field grazed my tomatoes had grown and flourished. It made me wonder why I had ever planted more than we could eat. But they had become tangled with weeds, and some were rotting. I weeded then pulled off the tomatoes that were too far gone and threw them in the dirt. When I looked behind me, my love, my silly little cocker spaniel and our peacock friend made me laugh. They were such an odd couple. I had been so lost in thought that I didn't look to see that they were right beside me. I was so appreciative for their company and wondered if they knew how much this simple moment meant to me.

My sweet little Stella Bella. She fell from the silver-screen classic *Lady and the Tramp* and found her way to my home and heart. She was my soulmate dog. We were so close, so connected that my illness had taken a toll on her too. She had gotten sick only months after my first procedure. I feared all the drama of my going in and out of the hospital and all the pain and bed rest had taken her health away. She had spent some time in the hospital herself with a parasite that almost killed her, and she lost 80 percent of her kidney function. She was on medication, and I often had to give her IV fluids.

I had a vet bill of close to five thousand dollars trying to keep her alive, plus the cost of medications and prescription food. Money which I didn't have because I was trying to keep myself alive and my family afloat. So I bartered with the vet for a portrait of his dogs. It was a tough commitment to keep, painting and then making the monthly payments for the difference, the food, and meds. It took me almost two years to complete the portraits and pay down the bill. I felt ashamed and embarrassed that it had taken so long but grateful that her life could be spared by the veterinary's compassion.

Henry the Peacock had come to my door over two years ago. He just showed up one day and adopted us and became part of our family. He was such a beauty with his opulent feathers and long, sparkling jewel of a tail. Often displaying them for us in the afternoon sun. He was right next to my little angel, a beautiful feast for the eyes.

Although I would never have thought that gardening would have been on the top of my list of things to do before I died. Oddly enough, it felt right. Stella and Henry had made my heavy heart and the day palatable. But then the enjoyment of the moment was short lived, as pain soon overtook me. A sharp, unpredictable pain that felt as if some unseen force had begun stabbing me in the right side of my abdomen. Small tears welled up in my eyes looking at the fading, burnt-orange light of the sunset.

I doubled over holding my breath. In those moments of anguish, I found it helpful to think of something, anything but the pain. With closed eyes I let my mind drift, reflecting on the garden. The tomatoes transported me to my father's death and how the tomatoes didn't grow that year he had passed. I could still see him so clearly during those last days in the ICU. I could remember almost word for word how we talk-ed about the tomatoes and gardening. It was then Stella came over and licked my face, giving me comfort and love, and I opened my eyes. In that moment I was thankful that Stella needed no words from me. Words got muddled with emotions. Words could be misunderstood or never said, as in the case of my father's death. It was hard not being able to save my father, and that still haunted me, still made me feel guilty that I never said all I wanted to say. Yet I thought, as I wiped my tears and held Stella in my arms, that I had learned so much about life and death from that time spent with my father in the hospital. I could appreciate that every day alive was precious and not to be wasted. My sadness of him dying so young had washed away. We would, I knew, always have the tomatoes and the love of nature, gardening, cooking, and learning—and that was a lot. It made me wonder how far back this green thumb went in our family's history. Was my love of the earth something inherited?

The spasm and intense pain faded to a dull ache, and I turned my attention back to the garden and my weeding. I felt at peace as I contemplated the abundance of growth which, I hoped, would be a good omen for me.

The next morning, around six AM, I sat in the blue velvet chair in my living room waiting for my ride to the hospital. The chair was one Stella sat in often, sharing it with me or one of my daughters and an array of animals that came in and out of the house. This day she sat on my lap looking weak, her eyes glazed over. She had rallied, as I did the day before. I had tried so hard to keep us healthy. But I was failing. I could see it as I looked into her eyes. I held her face close to mine. I felt her soft, warm fur and held her to me and whispered how much I loved her. Even though I wanted it not to be true, somehow I knew that I would never see her again.

The tears welled up. I had to tell her I was so sorry that I had to go. She would often stop eating when I was away. I had to say to her that she needed to eat when I left. It was words that I clung to in desperation, which only the day before I had felt were unnecessary. If they could only make a difference. It was as if she knew what no one else did. What I couldn't say to my child—wishing and torn between feeling my words useless but hoping they had the power to heal.

It was my fault. It was my fault for getting too attached to her and letting her get too attached to me. I reluctantly left for the hospital leaving her in the good, loving hands of my youngest daughter.

I went into surgery thinking of her and my girls. I thought of the black-and-white photo that hung on the wall in my hallway. It was one I took of the three of them outside next to the barn. It was a happier time and one of the photos of them I love the most. It helped me in that moment of fear as they started the IV, then gave me the anesthesia. But as I felt the sting of the drugs in my veins, I became troubled by a thought. What if I died while I was under, would I know I was dead? I reeled at the idea that I would be stuck in some strange limbo forever walking the earth as a ghost not knowing who or where I was.

I forced my eyes to stay open as my body disappeared into a heavy sleep. I tasted the drugs in my mouth and wanted to call out, *No. Stop. I changed my mind, let me go.* But it was too late, and my eyes were too heavy. I disappeared into a wave of darkness and a dull, unnatural humming drove me down into a bottomless tunnel, a limbo of nothingness.

When I became conscious, I didn't remember the surgery.

I couldn't open my eyes, but I heard a distant angelic music—I thought angels were singing.

Was I dead? No, I couldn't be since the pain shimmered through my body.

I couldn't speak, only listen, and I listened to the singing and talking of the running machines. I wanted to shut it all out. I wanted to disappear back into the darkness of anesthesia.

But the nurse wouldn't let me and shook me awake. She called my name, asked me to speak. When I could finally form a word, it was the word *pain*.

They gave me more morphine. I disappeared for a while.

I woke in excruciating pain and with questions that never made it out of my mouth. Had they given me anything? Why was I being tortured? And why were they singing?

Then I heard someone say it was terrible that the pope had died. The pope had passed away, and they were having his funeral. It was on the TV. It wasn't angels singing it was humans that sounded like angels.

I lived and the pope had died. Why did he have to die, and how was I still alive?

Then as my pain grew, I asked a nurse for some more pain medication.

"If I give you any more you'll be with the pope."

Her words repeated in my head like one of the parrots I'd sat for.

I thought that wouldn't be so bad. I'd just go back to sleep not feeling anything. I was done and just wanted to disappear. I couldn't stand to be in this body anymore.

But they wouldn't let me go back to sleep. They kept waking me, talking to me, and when they touched me, it made my skin crawl. I couldn't have anybody touch me. Every inch of my body screamed with pain. Every cell shouted and cried with horror.

When I was moved to my room the misery continued to grow. Injections in my stomach for blood clots. I then developed internal bleeding, pancreatitis again, and pneumonia. I laid there, unable to move, wishing for it all to be over, for my life to end.

If anyone came to see me, I didn't remember. Only Julianne who came and told me stories. She sat by my side and touched my arm, and it felt like she was touching an open wound.

The sound of her voice permeated the darkness I fell into, her voice so far away as if playing on a distant radio. My baby girl was probably scared, and all I could think of was that I wanted life to be over. How could I be so selfish?

She told me a story that she'd made up, as I had done for her so many times before she would fall asleep as a child. I tried to listen and hold on to every word, like I was climbing up the loose rocks on the edge of a cliff.

My eyes opened momentary. My body could hardly move. Yet I wanted to tell her I was still there, that I was listening.

Although I couldn't move or speak, she knew must have known I could hear because she went on. I don't know what the story was about or how long it went on for, I could only remember one thing about that day that made me want to try. She stopped and leaned in so close I could feel her breath on my cheek, and she whispered: "Don't leave me alone."

She knew I wanted to go, but she needed me to stay.

Don't leave me alone. The words echoed in my mind like a steel ball being bounced around a pinball machine.

Don't leave me alone. It touched the nerve of emotions that had been doused and suffocated by morphine and Demerol.

Don't leave me alone. It was my own silent plea as a child living in unpredictable chaos. It made me feel the days when I was helpless and rocked myself to sleep pleading to God, *Don't leave me alone.*

A few days later, when I was able to talk, Melissa called and the nurse held the phone to my ear. "Stella, how is she?" I asked.

"She's not good, Mom."

I knew what was happening, that my Stella was dying, and I was in the hospital trying to survive. I wanted to go home to be with her. But how could I if I couldn't even sit up or hold any food down?

I began willing myself better. I wanted to leave to be with Stella. Then there was what Julianne said to me. She didn't know that I'd heard her that day, and I never told her I did. But I knew no matter how hard or painful it was I had to try.

I was still weak but became stable, and the internal bleeding had stopped. I still had pancreatitis and pneumonia and was in great pain. But I was going to recover. How long I cannot remember, only that when I could finally sit up, I asked to be discharged. My doctor wanted me to stay longer, but Stella was fading, and I needed to be with her.

Against my doctor's recommendation I checked myself out of the hospital.

Maybe I could do for Stella what Julianne had done for me and whisper in Stella's ear, *Don't leave me alone.* We could try together.

I waited to be unplugged from the IV and monitoring machines and to be discharged. There was a growing feeling of desperation, for Stella needed me.

It took me so long to get dressed and even longer waiting for my ride. But right before I left to go home, I got the phone call that Stella was gone. She had died in her bed. Rushing home early to be with her, to try and save her, was in vain. Grief overcame me. In my bed filled with tears I put the morphine patch on, took my medication, and closed my eyes. I wanted the silence, the emptiness to take me away.

A few days later, it was late at night, and my bedroom door was open. In the faint light I saw her in the hallway walking to my room. I called out to her. "Stella? Stella?" But she faded away, and so did I, into a deep, dark sleep. I saw her a few more times and even heard her walking around as she had for the last five years. She came to me in a dream wagging her little stump of a tail. But as I reached for her, I woke up violently, choking and coughing. After that dream I tried to get up to go to the bathroom. Walking from my bed to the bathroom only a few feet away, weak and in pain, I thought of a woman I didn't know but who was close to my age. She was a patient of my doctor who was in the same hospital at the same time and for the same surgery. She had died a short while after I had left the hospital. It brought home the reality of how close I had come to dying and the question of why.

Why me? Why was I spared but left so debilitated?

That, and the loss of Stella, ran through my mind as I struggled holding on to the wall. "You can make it," I said. But I didn't make it and collapsed on the cold hardwood floor in the hallway. Tears ran from my eyes for my loss and humiliation of the body I felt trapped in. Too weak to move, I passed out. When I woke up it was dark outside. I realized I have been laying there for hours. A thought came to mind as I crawled back to bed: how on earth would I ever get out of this?

CHAPTER 17:
FINDING HOPE ON FEATHERED WINGS

The big trip from the bedroom to check the heat left me out of breath, and I sunk deep into the pillows and blankets on the overstuffed couch.

The thermostat had said it was well over seventy degrees in the house, but I didn't believe it, as I was still shivering, and my hands and feet felt like icicles.

It might have been a few years since my first procedures, but I couldn't remember, nor did I want to anymore, as I was no closer to feeling better.

Winter had made everything harder. Melissa moved to Denver, and I missed her. Julianne was always out with friends. The medication I was on wasn't really helping and was causing bone loss, and I was afraid I would break something.

Spending my time in bed or on the couch, staring out the window, had become my life. Just to wipe the snow from the truck was enough to send me back to bed. Cold, exhausted, nauseated, defeated. An empty vessel filled with misery, afraid to leave the house. Being out in public I never knew when I would have a bout of crippling pain or fatigue.

When things were good, I had saved some money. Now It was mostly gone. The bills piled up on my desk, unopened, while I kept falling down into a pit of fogginess.

Hopeless about what to do, I shut down and turned on the television. Wanting to get lost in something other than my problems. There was a show on about penguins and how they lived and survived the harsh artic winters. Not the best choice for the way I was feeling. The penguins huddled together as I reminisced. Recalling my twenties and how I had worked carving a penguin and an artist's life. Using a tall cardboard box, I had filled it with plaster of Paris. How I had loved the warm energy generated by the white powder and water as it turned solid.

When I tore away the cardboard, I saw a penguin hidden, waiting to be set free. Chiseling away, someone in the studio asked why I had chosen to sculpt a penguin. All I could think was that's what it said it needed to be. It made me wonder; could I set myself free from this icy block of time I was frozen in? Could I carve myself out as I had the penguin or paint a summer filled with wildflowers? These questions had been looming. For too long now I had asked with no answers, the silence torturing.

My eyes wandered around the room. Catching my attention were two paintings leaning on the windowsills. I had put them there a few years back for a touch of spring on a winter's day. In crisp, white frames sat wildflowers, yellow black-eyed Susans, and purple deadly nightshades without any spirit of what I felt when I had painted them.

In the corner of the room, cast in bronze and collecting dust, sat my *Dare to Dream* sculpture. The strong, muscular horse's head facing down, eyes up, ready to throw his head back in joy. He had large open wings, one foot on the ground and the others in the air. It was a piece I had done a few years ago, when I was feeling like I could do anything.

As I stared at the little reminders of the nature I loved around me, instead of joy or pride I could only feel resentment for the memories. The awards I had won for it and the art shows I had done was a distant dream.

When I first got sick, I had put up a bird feeder outside the living room window. As I wasn't able to go hiking to see them for such a long time, I had hoped the birds would come to visit me. Luring them with sunflower and millet seeds. I had raised most of the species that had come. Chickadees, tufted titmouse, nut-hatchers, house finches, mourning doves, catbirds, mockingbirds, blue jays, and cardinals.

Except today, there were very few birds as the snow fell, and most of the trees were gone.

Lonely for the life I had built, holding on to myself, my work felt like I was trying to hold water in my hands. Except for a drop or two, the life-giving liquid was slipping away.

The snow started coming down heavy. The large flakes looked like the ones the girls and I would cut out of paper when they were little. Preferring to stare out the window I clicked off the TV. It was giving me a headache anyway. The stains from the leaky roof in my living room started to weep with water. It seemed as if it was taking forever for some-one to come and fix it. It felt like the carriage house was crying too.

It was last summer when the landlord had called to tell me he had sold the estate, something he would later regret.

"Will we have to move? I love it here. It's the best place I've ever been."

"Well, then you've never been anywhere."

Those words stuck with me. And I replayed them in my head a million times. Like lyrics in a song, I was trying to grasp the meaning. After I thanked him for telling me and being so kind to me and my children, I apologized. Embarrassed by my crying. I cried all the time as my hormones were on a roller-coaster ride of emotions. Up sometimes—but mostly down. It was a combination of the liver damage and an over or underactive thyroid; I can't remember which. With no sleep and chronic pain, I had lost all control.

Not long after, the new owners of the estate moved in.

I was grateful I could stay but was on edge since it was a month-to-month lease. And if I had to leave in my state, where were we to go?

The new owners were wealthy, unfriendly people and took over the land like a punishing storm. They owned a chain of laundromats, making their money one quarter at a time. They kicked out all the horses that boarded there, including JoJo. The animals they brought to the farm were disturbed. All the horses were distrusting, and the white horse they'd brought to the barn would try to bite anyone who walked by. The barn became overrun with rats, and I no longer visited it or the horses.

The new owners wasted no time cutting down almost all the trees in favorer of rows of neatly trimmed grass. I cried during the long days when the chainsaws buzzed away. For the trees, for the birds, for all that had been lost. The mourning doves that sat and cooed outside my bedroom window for so many years had lost their home. They had raised their young in that tree, and I worried for them. Where would they go? I didn't see them anymore. My grief overwhelmed me and felt as if someone I'd loved had just died.

Their boxer ran amuck and bit his own owner, then killed my peacock, Henry. It happened last summer when I wanted to have my tea outside and get some fresh air. Henry, who would wait outside the door for me, wasn't there. I wondered if he missed Stella as much as I did and where he was. Then I saw a feather of his long, beautiful tail, then another. I followed the trail of feathers in horror.

Then I found him.

Dead on the new green sod, the boxer over him, wagging his tail for the life he took.

"Go home!" I yelled in tears, and the dog ran back to the big yellow house.

I picked up Henry. Sobbing, I buried him next to my garden, stopping only to catch my breath and rest. Then went back to collect his feathers and bought them into the house, putting them in a vase like flowers and sitting them in the corner of my room.

After JoJo was moved he got colic, and I heard he had to be put down. It happened shortly after a hospital stay, so I was still recovering and didn't get to say goodbye. I didn't get to tell him how much I had loved him. Again, there was no closure, just moving on. I had heard he wasn't letting anyone ride him for a while. It pained me so. He must have thought I had abandoned him. I was missing everyone I loved. Then the new landlord raised the rent, and for the first time in over five year since I moved to the carriage house, I was late paying it.

The place I had loved so much had become a place of pain.

One male cardinal showed up in the hour I sat watching. The wind picked up, and it was snowing hard. It was then that a tufted titmouse braved the storm. He was on his own and pushed the snow away with his beak. As he ate a hawk swooped down out of nowhere and slammed the open wooded bird feeder into the side of the house. It made a loud whack, and I jumped up. He snatched the tiny bird in his sharp talons and flew off. Surprised, I pressed my nose against the window to see. I had never witnessed a hawk hunt in such weather.

I grabbed my binoculars from the windowsill. The drama played out in slow motion as the hawk flew off with its prize. The little bird struggled to get free, flapping its wings, feathers flying everywhere.

I thought he was done for. My heart raced as the tufted titmouse struggled to free himself from the hawk's grasp! Eventually he slipped out! He had saved himself! He was free! He flew away to the safety of the tree line at the end of the property.

With the lost element of surprise, the hawk flew off without trying to recapture his prey.

The little bird sat still and quiet in the tree as I did in my house. The small bird's survival surprisingly felt like my own victory. It became mine as I had emotionally connected to the cold, the fear of death and this solitary battle.

The little bird fluffed his feathers. Was he checking to see if he had any injuries? Was he worried that the hawk would come back to finish him off? He began preening himself, and a few more feathers fell out. He stayed still for a moment longer, looking around, clearly shaken up. Then he fluffed his feathers up and smoothed them down again. He took flight, heading straight toward me! I put the binoculars down. My heart raced. I froze. I didn't want to move and scare him away. I wanted to look into his eyes. I wanted to see the truth of his being.

Only a few inches from me on the other side of the window, trying to keep still, I found myself holding my breath as I looked into his eyes.

He had come back to the bird feeder and begun to eat as if nothing had happened. He was almost killed. Yet he came back to the place where he was most exposed. He came back to living. I wanted to see.

Did he have fear? If he did, he didn't show it. It was cold, and the trees were bare and the ground covered in deep snow.

Maybe his heart was beating a mile a minute, like mine, but he didn't show it.

He opened my eyes to the struggle of life. It was everywhere.

It made me think of what his life was like, living in a tree with only his feathers to keep him warm. He was a real survivor. He moved on and lived his best life, despite the danger.

I got it. If this tiny bird could find a way to get on with living, even in the face of death, against the odds, then why the hell couldn't I? I became ashamed of myself for accepting the way things were. For not trying harder. For not rising to the new challenges I faced.

I thought how birds were really so amazing. I summoned the dreams I used to have of flying. So inspirational, cathartic, freeing.

One of the biggest declines in bird population is loss of habitat. Something I was seeing firsthand. What could I do to help? What could I do to say thank you to that little bird?

I pondered for days.

Collecting dust in a pile of unread mail and bills was a grant application. The grant was for a project that would somehow benefit and educate the community. I had hated that the new owners had cut all the old-growth trees away on the property, and for what? Acres of grass that had to be watered and mowed. Perhaps I could do an art project? Paintings of birds to bring awareness about their loss of habitat and share it with the community—for me and for the birds.

It would be perfect if I could do an art show at the wildlife sanctuary. So I called the new director. She loved the idea, and I pulled myself together the best I could to meet with her about the details. Now I had something else to think about besides my own despair. It would give a real purpose to my day.

Filling out the grant application with dyslexia and sitting in a hard chair occupied with pain was a struggle. Yet as I wrote about a secret garden with the beautiful songs from the birds, I regained all the love and passion I had inside for nature. And when it got hard or the pain too deep, I thought of that little bird, and it helped me through.

I had to drop off the grant application the day it was due. On the way I pulled over my SUV at least three times to rest. With the clock ticking I arrived within an hour of the deadline.

It had taken so much out of me to put it together that I spent the next few days in bed recovering. I thought I probably wouldn't get the grant anyway. But that would be okay, as it made me feel alive again just to try.

A month or so later the mail came and with it was a letter from the grant committee.

With butterflies in my stomach, I propped the letter against the vase on the kitchen table. I stared at it for a while, then out the window, before opening it. I took a deep breath in apprehension. Winning, no matter how small, was still a possibility. Rejection, no matter how many times I had faced it and accepted it, would still sting.

When I opened the letter, I had to read it twice before I could understand and absorb the meaning. I had won! How wonderful that others cared about the birds as I did. What a validation for my new mission.

Some cultures, including the Cherokee Indians, believe that birds are considered messengers for the spirit world.

The message was clear to me: love of one's work and creating a better world for others was the air under my wings, lifting me up to higher places and loftier goals.

CHAPTER 18:

EXCAVATING A PROMISED LIFE

Heading my way at full speed down the long hallway was a powder-blue-and-white parakeet. He looked like a small paper airplane. Hot on his tail was a gang of production assistants, cameramen, and set designers. The crew looked as if they were fleeing from a fire. Amusement and panic struck me, yet I remained composed and professional.

No doubt the bird was camera shy, and flying away from his television debut was something I could relate to.

I was back working on the set of the *Martha Stewart Show*. It was during a lunch break that I had slipped away for a short rest in my car when the bird snuck out.

It was nice to be back and visit with my coworkers, and it was funny to see them running. Going back to work, even part-time, was a challenge. But I *had* to work. I had saved some money for emergencies, but that was all gone now. The grant for my art project on migratory birds covered little more than the cost of materials and travel.

Without a misstep or blink of an eye, I kept my pace as the group shouted and waved to me as if I didn't see the bird heading my way. I was calculating the right moment to make my move. I waited until the small bird got close. As he folded his wings, and just before he opened them again, I plucked him from the air.

"Hi baby, where are you going to? It's not an actual house," I said, rubbing his head, and he chirped back. I looked up and announced to the crew, "It's okay, I got him. I'll put him back."

Everyone cheered in relief, and for a moment, I thought the crew was going to carry me away on their shoulders. It made me feel like a kid who hit the home run and won the game for my team. The story lived on for months in the studio. I was back, a bird-plucking hero or, as Martha would call me, the "Bird Wrangler."

I had evolved and developed a talent that would make my totem bird, the peregrine falcon, proud.

When not on the set working, I was immersed in the wild. The world of birds and a hotline for rare-bird sightings became my obsession. I would call the hotline almost every day.

Going out and spending my days, often walking or sitting for hours looking for that elusive, flying, mysterious traveler, sometimes going home without seeing the bird I was looking for. Other times it was an abundance of sightings that filled my notebook and sketchbook.

One cold winter day, I heard there was a sighting of a snowy owl. It was on top of my list to see in the wild. Even though I despised the cold, I bundled up and went searching on the beach. Excited, I walked up and down half the day looking; the beach was empty, except for a few seagulls. Disappointed, tired, and freezing, my body was craving a warm bed and a hot cup of tea. But right as I was leaving, the dreamy pastel sunset caused me to pause. As I lingered, the snowy owl landed on the dune in front of me! Incredible! It was as if to say, look at me, I'm as breathtaking as the sunset, and he was! It was one of my most sensational sightings.

"Thank you," I whispered as I stood like a statue until it got dark and the white ghost of an owl flew away. Even though I didn't get any good photos of the owl, as the lighting was too poor, the memory of the owl and sunset would stay in my mind. I could already see the finished painting on canvas with its soft edges and muted colors.

As I sat in the car shivering, waiting for the heat to come on, my mind was busy painting as pain and fatigue flooded my body like a dam breaking open. It made me note the time spent focused on searching for the owl, doing what felt important and what I loved. My pain seemed to dissipate. I wasn't sure if it was gone for that time or if I wasn't aware of it as much; however, this relief was short-lived. Still, it made me believe there was a hidden power to be found. One that could heal the body and spirit. It was in these moments when my mind focused on my work that I almost forgot about my discomfort. Not every time, but I thought if it could happen once, then maybe I could find the key to make my pain go away for good.

My time in nature became part of my healing process. It was hard at first and was kind of like meditating. I had meditated at home or in a class. But this was different. At home, after all the medical procedures, I had trouble concentrating and had the attention span of a toddler. That was slowly changing with my new project and so much time spent outdoors.

It took an entire year's worth of work to have my first exhibit in a long time. Paintings I did were of owls, falcons, hawks, warbles, and colorful birds, like the indigo bunting. A bright-blue, small, stocky, sparrow-like bird.

Beside the art were some framed photographs I took and a photo documentary slideshow.

When opening night at the wildlife sanctuary finally came, I was a bundle of nerves, as over a hundred guests were invited. All of my work was on exhibit to be seen, to be judged. I wasn't sure if it was me feeling insecure about the exhibit or because it was raining so hard. Would anyone even show up? I was even questioning the impact the work would have on them if they did.

That day, before the guests arrived, I looked around at my work and wished I could have painted more than I did. But the work went slow as I painted between days of bed rest and trying to earn a living. I had to talk myself down from the negative spiral I was falling into. If anyone showed up, I needed to be relaxed and attentive so I could share what I had learned. It was also important because I was donating a percentage of the sales to the sanctuary. I wanted them to be happy with the results. So I kept my nerves busy by fussing over the details, such as the labels and cards with the story of that bird species next to the artwork. The birds I painted sat quietly on the walls while I checked each one. As I stood back, the work collectively spoke to me.

It made me stop and take in the art and the memories of all my encounters.

It calmed me down, and I took a long, deep breath and sighed out my worries.

Moving across the hall to do a test run of my photo documentary, I rearranged the chairs, lining them up in several rows as the staff put on some classical music I had requested that would play on a loop. Making sure it was playing in sync with the photos, I sat down to experience it as the viewer, not the creator.

It needed something, but what? Then it came to me.

It would have more of an impact if the room was dark. So I shut the lights off to give the sensation of an intimate movie theater.

Then I saw it—the tufted titmouse in the slides, and I teared up. The day of seeing the tufted titmouse swindle death had kept me going.

The year I spent working on the bird project I was also working on improving my health. Pushing myself harder than I had ever done before. I found new doctors and had a new agenda. I was weaning myself off some of the medication, opting for natural alternatives. It was a slow process, but I was patient and willing to do whatever it took.

Working with a nutritional biologist, I tried acupuncture and acupressure therapy and even cupping treatments. I would try just about anything looking for answers. Some helped, some didn't. Sometimes I tried to barter for artwork.

There was scar tissue the doctor said was pulling on the surrounding tissues of my stomach and nerve endings and was part of what I was told caused me pain when I moved around and engaged my stomach muscles. The months of bed rest had left me weak and out of breath just walking across the hall or going up the stairs.

Then a friend's boyfriend, who was a brilliant personal trainer, came to my house and worked with me once a week on a sliding scale. He took what I could afford, and sometimes it was barely gas money. But each week he came with creative ways for me to build strength in my body, working around the movements that would cause me to at times collapse in agony.

Educating myself during my bed rest I devoured as many health books as I could. When sent to a pain-management clinic I opted for biofeedback over painkillers that would surely lead to brain fog and addiction. I had to be resourceful, as my bank account was mostly empty. Growing up poor and going to college on a tight budget refined these skills. There were other skill sets I didn't even know I had that I was discovering every day.

At work, the long days were almost too much, but it was nice to be working back on a set. It was also nice that no one, except for a close friend who was a cameraman at PBS and Martha Stewart, knew of my health struggles. Sometimes on the way to work I would still have to pull over. There were days I cried or yelped because of a sudden sharp pain. It would come and go in waves, as if some invisible being were stabbing me in my side or punching me in the stomach. It would take my breath away, and I often felt betrayed by my body, as I was working so hard to care for it. Taking supplements and drinking things that were good for me but made me gag.

Very few, outside of close friends and family, knew of my struggles. It made me feel normal, like I would be okay, that I could live a regular life, and those moments were precious. The night of the art show was like the day at the *Martha Stewart Show* studio. There was pride in my step. No one at the sanctuary knew of what I had gone through to get here.

As I walked back to the room where the art was on display, there was a man with two young girls studying a small owl portrait I had done. I heard the little girl say, "Yes, Daddy, that's the one." She couldn't have been more than seven or eight.

The man turned and said, "Hi. We can't make it to the show to-night, but we'd like to buy this one now, if we can. My daughter loves it. We're fine leaving it here until the show's over."

I felt a little red in the cheeks, smiled, and said, "I'll get someone for you."

I walked out of the room and got one of the staff members.

"Hey," I said. "There's someone who would like to buy a painting now."

She smiled, winked, and said, "I'll be right in," then did a wiggle dance.

I went back in, and the girl looked as if they she was getting a big ice cream cone or a horse. I couldn't imagine what that must have felt like at that age, for your dad to buy an original painting for you. I discreetly wiped my sweaty hand on my pants before I offered it up to shake.

"She'll be right in," I said. "And I'm the artist, if you have any questions."

We talked for a while, and I was grateful for the test run.

That night, I felt like a princess at a coming-out ball. The art show/fundraiser was a tremendous success. With a full house, we sold most of my work, and it made me feel like everything would be all right. People had brought me flowers, and the project made all the local papers. I even did some local television interviews. It was more than I could ask for—for me and my feathered friends and the sanctuary.

Pleased with the success of my project, the grant committee gave me a grant for the following year. The Audubon Center asked to use my research material for their educational programs. Then the governor sent a representative and awarded me a certificate of achievement and contributions for my work in the arts.

Mary would have loved it, and I was missing her being there.

A few days later the director of the sanctuary said the *New York Times* wanted to interview me for the Sunday edition.

"Really?" I gasped in disbelief.

I met the reporter at the sanctuary and showed her the work, and we sat and talked. It didn't feel like an interview at all. A photographer showed up and photographed me with the peregrine falcon I had painted a few years back. It didn't feel real, and I could hardly wait to see the paper. So, Saturday night I headed out to pick up the paper at midnight. My friend worked at the late-night luncheonette that I once waitressed at years and years before. I would still go there sometimes to see her and have tea and talk.

Anxiously, I asked as I waved hello, "Did you read it?"

She nodded, and her smile widened. "I saved a few for you."

"Was it okay?" I said with a lump in my throat.

She said nothing but, "Tea?"

That told me it was good and I should just read it for myself. She knew me well, had been like a sister since forever, and our daughters were like cousins. She put out the tea, then poured hot water in my cup as I sat down. Then she put the papers in front of me. I put my hand on it to feel it first before opening it.

After taking a deep breath, I opened it and looked up at my friend and said, "Wow."

There it was, in black and white, calling me a modern-day Audubon.

"I know," she said. "I'm so proud of you."

It felt strange to read about myself. I did something. I had made and kept promises to myself and the wildlife I loved.

Not long after I flew from New York to Denver, where Melissa was living. Wanting to spend some time together we planned to drive back to New York by way of Yellowstone. This trip was going to be a real test for my body, and that was the challenge for me, to overcome a deep fear I had developed of not going too far from home. I was so fearful for so long of getting sick or having an overcoming pain in public that it kept me from going. It was well and good to traipse around Long Island, then run home if the pain or fatigue became too much. Also, this would be a test for my bigger dream of going to Africa. If I could do this, then maybe one day.

I was dusting off some of my dreams, and it felt good to have hope and joy in my life again.

We stayed in a cabin in the park, and my first wildlife encounter was a visit in the middle of the night by a mouse who played pop goes the weasel in our bag of groceries. We were first frightened by the noise, then laughed at the small intruder.

I couldn't sleep in anticipation of what might find the next morning. An entire world of wild, free animals was just outside the door.

Before sunrise, my daughter gave in with a sigh. "I can hear you waiting. I know you want to go, so let's go."

"Are you sure?" I was giddy. She knew how much being in and around wildlife in their natural environment made me feel like a child.

My landlord's words rang out in my head: *Then you've never been anywhere.*

"Well, here I go," I murmured back.

I had a mental list of things I wanted to experience there. Number one was to horseback ride to the top of the Tetons. Except for short walks hiking wasn't something I could manage yet. Horseback riding would be a good way to cover more ground where the car couldn't go.

We drove in the morning fog. The enormous bison walked past us on the road, so close I could have reached out and touched them. But would never even try, as they were wild and we were in their space and they deserved respect.

Even being so close the small eyes within the primitive herds were hard to see within their massive, wooly, brown heads. It made me wonder how they thought.

As I watched them my mind couldn't help but wander to their predators. Man and the wolf were the first to come to mind.

I had once cared for an Arctic wolf and had watched him grow from a small pup to a grown wolf. We were good friends, and I loved our time together. He was as curious about me as I was about him. The wolf, as he grew, would stop and look at my sketchbook as I scratched the paper with my pencils, always putting my book away as soon as I was done. One day I had laid down the sketchbook for a moment, and he stole it and ran, refusing to give it back. It took the rest of the day to find a suitable trade with him, from food to chew toys. He left me a present of a bite out of the corner. I smile thinking of him every time I take out that book.

But now I wanted to see his relatives in the wild. To see and know that they were free and to do something for them to help keep it that way in a promise I had made to my wolf friend.

I got my wish. I saw them from a distance as the pack studied the elk. Melissa and I stood on the side of the road in the openness of Lamar Valley. The wolves were far away, but I could still feel them. My brain was on fire with sparks of creativity. The next day, as we mounted the horses, I tried to hold every bit of light and the long afternoon shadows, composing and painting in my mind as we rode.

I held on to air that smelled of pine and felt clean and alive with it.

It was a life-changing trip and a missed opportunity to fulfill a dream, as I found out when I came home to a missed call from a billionaire for whom I had animal-sat for a few years. He had wanted me to take two hound-dog puppies to his estate in Kenya for him on his private plane with a stopover in Paris and a free plane ticket home.

I hadn't been anywhere in such a long time, and it had to be on this wonderful trip that I missed one of my biggest dreams. What were the chances of this happening? I was out of town, and he couldn't hold the plane any longer. It was heartbreaking, and I could have never in my wildest dreams thought that a trip to Africa on a private plane would ever be an option. I took it as a reminder that anything is possible.

I could have dwelled on the lost opportunity but instead decided to fulfill one of my other oldest dreams. It was what I had hoped for everyday as a child—to live in the country. It was then I knew I would need to go back to the place that that dream was born in order to go fully forward.

Back to Brooklyn and the house that I often visited in my sleep.

CHAPTER 19:
DESTINY'S ROSE GARDEN

It had been over twenty years since my father had passed. Well over thirty years since I had seen the house I was born in. The house was gone. Torn down in favor of a fast-food restaurant. Yet, some part of me believed it would still be here. That somehow, like me, it would have survived.

Coming back to this place, I knew was inevitable, it was just a matter of when.

After I parked the car and stepped out in front of where my house once stood, a wave of tears filled my eyes. It was a relief that no one was there to see me cry. It felt as if some unseen force had cleared the space for me to explore and grieve with the little girl of my past.

It was in the early afternoon, and I was standing at the back of a parking lot in Brooklyn. Staring at the hamburger restaurant as if it was an invasive parasite that had eaten the house the house I grew up in and had vanished. All that was left was cold concrete and processed meat.

Even though I felt ready to come here, my stomach turned with anxiousness. I realized I was looking for something tangible. Something that would tell me this wasn't a dream place. I questioned how I could still make peace with this place and its memories.

I would have to. I had come too far, and this journey was a necessary part of my evolution. I looked to the ground and closed my watery eyes and called on the strongest part of my memory to conjure a ghost house.

I took a deep breath and exhaled the present in exchange for a glimpse into the past. In it I imagined stepping through the gate of my home.

Walking up the concrete steps to the stoop, there it was in small moments of clarity and passing confusion. Was the stoop green or gray? I tried to recall, but all I could see in my mind's eye was the chipped and peeling paint. There was the small black metal mailbox to my right stuffed with overdue bills. To my left, overgrown weeds. In the mist of the banged-up tin garbage cans that overflowed with garbage, I could almost see it, smell it. The smells mixed with the pizza place that had been next door.

I looked up at the underside of the overhang canopy to my room that was right above it. In my mind's eye I opened the heavy double-wooded glass doors. I remembered the key that I had tucked in my shirt to let myself in after school. It hung around my neck on a string for years, like a necklace.

It felt so real as I counted the steps. I walked through the ghost of a house.

I recalled the small foyer that was tiled with a black-and-white mosaic pattern. It had always caught my eye. The workmanship and details of the house and church were one thing I marveled at, something the artist inside me always appreciated.

As I looked down the narrow hallway, I could see myself, the child I once was. Splitting myself in two to become the strong woman I was now, no longer that sad, lonely child. I could feel the hurts and fears and saw myself holding her hand in comfort. We sat together on the staircase listening to the futile fighting of my parents that had gone on for years.

We walked together past the curved staircase that kept a broken bronze statue that once held a light I never saw. I could almost touch the smooth wooden banister, remembering how unsuccessfully I would try to slide down it.

I wiped my tears.

I stopped at the door to the downstairs apartment. It was heavy with a sturdy lock. To the left was the thin door to the dirt cellar, its lock a flimsy hook-and-eye with a tarnished brass doorknob that often entered my dreams and fears. It caused me to pause. A chill went up my spine, and I shook it off and drew my attention to the imagined spot where the kitchen would be.

Ironically, measuring the things I hated about this place helped me to remember the good times and things I had once loved there. Balancing them as one would balance coal and golden nuggets on a scale of justice. How much bad versus how much good? I had to look hard, but I found a few pieces of gold. Those would be the ones I would move on with. I could almost see the antique clock that sat silent on the cold white marble fireplace.

Our home was a two-family house in a double lot with a small yard and a garden of roses.

I counted the steps in the parking lot to where I imagined the backyard to be, where the rose bushes once were. The roses were gone too. And for what? In favor of a slap of uninspiring concrete. If anything were here, I wish it would have been the roses.

Those roses were the nicest and biggest I had ever seen. A memory came back of my father's friend talking to me in our kitchen. It was a story he had told me as a child as I arranged the large fragrant roses of soft pink and pale yellow. I listened as I placed the flowers in a clear-cut glass in an ancient vase. It was a vase I had imagined my great-grandmother or great-aunts had once used. As my hands throbbed from the pricks of sharp thorns he told the story of how my grandfather had won an award for his roses. He watched me as he sipped his beer and remarked on how I seemed to care for them and how it reminded him of my grandfather. With eyes closed, even though I couldn't remember what he looked like, I could still see my grandfather standing there in his prime, a proud gardener.

How was the love of roses mine alone, or was it inherited from him? Their perfume was so strong and musty. The smell of them will live in my psyche forever. And although I tried, I never found such a rose that smelled like them again. To me, they were a symbol of hope. A garden in a place that had forgotten nature.

It was as if my grandfather had planted hope for us in the roses in what seemed a hopeless world. His time was during the Great Depression. His victory garden became my plea for brightness in a world blind to the light and healing power of nature.

I frowned at the concrete as I thought more about them.

I thought of how I had buried Destiny, my pet alligator, under those rose bushes. Putting him in an old tin box I'd found in the cellar. I wrapped him up like a mummy. I could remember the old white handkerchief that Nanny, my father's aunt, had given me for Christmas. The handkerchief was delicate with small embroidered flowers. I had used it to bury my Destiny. The soft, warm fabric was such a contrast to the scales of the cold alligator skin. Destiny had died right before the roses bloomed.

My father had given me Destiny for me for my ninth birthday. It was rare that my father would buy a gift for anyone, and I cannot remember him ever getting me anything else as a child.

Destiny's kaleidoscope eyes would memorize me, but his slit of black gave nothing away. He would stare at me, and I would look back, trying to communicate telepathically as I did with the dog and cat. Sitting with him for long periods of time, waiting for something to happen. Asking questions about how he was feeling. I wanted to see through his eyes. What was it like to be him? I was eleven when Destiny died.

When he passed, I had already been falling into deep depressions. His death was devastating. My tears flowed like acid rain. Ripping out a piece of paper from my school notebook, I marked down the date that Destiny had died. I even wrote him a poem that I put in his makeshift coffin, along with other things, like small tokens of meaning. My own time capsule. I couldn't remember any of the items I had placed in the box. It was a blur, an outline in the back of my mind of colors and shapes. Maybe a penny and a marble and something else. I could almost see it. I looked down now and examined the concrete as if it was there. Was he still here, or had he been ripped away by a bulldozer? I marveled at the idea of someone finding that rusty old box and the scribbles. The bad spelling of an eleven-year-old girl, a baby alligator buried in Brooklyn. Destiny, what a strange name for a strange pet I'd had so long ago. Destiny, it was in my hands now. What I did or didn't do was up to me, and this was the last bit of the past I would put to bed.

I turned and sighed at the junkyard that had once held a house on the other side of the double lot. Not to my surprise, the junkyard was still here. The house that had once stood on the back of the lot burned down when I was small. The one room left standing had become my playhouse. The land had become our junkyard, filled with rusted trucks and discarded junk, motors from vending machines my father would cut open with a blowtorch for their copper as I watched. I still had the small scars from falling into the burring pile of steaming motors. It happened when I was four or five. I could recall how funny I thought it was when my father hosed me down as he did the motors.

I stood staring into the junkyard a little longer before walking to the church, to my school, to find the pieces of me I had left there.

Bowing my head as I entered, I made the sign of the cross. Something I had done every day for years without thinking about it. My hand moved thoughtfully across my body as if it was collecting a lost penny of cellular memories.

The church was empty and as quiet as the sunlight that shone through the stained-glass windows. It was as I remembered—a colorful, tragic visual of the crucifixion. It would forever play out in those beautiful colored windows. The ones I studied almost every day for years.

They were here, and I felt my shoulders fall with relief. It was real, not a dream, and I was grateful that it was still intact.

Engrossed by the details, colors, artwork, and the story it told, I lingered, as I had done so many times before. Time itself became lost to me. The benches I would sometimes oil still smelled of pine as if I had just cleaned them. The smooth surface begged to be touched, so I sat down and listened to the organ playing in my mind from the balcony. Except for the altar, it all looked the same. It was overpowering to see it again.

When I finally walked out of the empty church, there were two women talking in the doorway. I was afraid they would ask me what I was doing there.

"Hi," I blurted, still in a trance from my pilgrimage. "I used to go to school and church here when it was St. Benedict's, a long time ago"

"Is that so?" one woman said with a smile. "We work in the school. It's different now."

"I know," I told her. "But the church is the same."

Although I didn't know if the school was different, as I hadn't been inside. I wanted to go in but then thought it was better if I didn't. I still had to go to the cemetery, and it was getting late. Feeling overwhelmed and faint, I wanted to leave. I wasn't sure why I was feeling this was until I glanced over to the courtyard.

"I was one of the last students here on the year it closed. I wanted to see it again." I said, looking away.

"Yeah," she said, nodding. "Now and then, someone stops by and says they went to school here and wants to see inside."

"Well, thank you," I said "It was nice meeting you."

I walked away, stopping at the courtyard for a few minutes to look around.

The basketball hoop had graffiti and no net.

I shivered as a chill passed over my body. It nauseated me. I put my head down in a silent prayer for the young man who was shot here. Often, I had wondered about him. He had died so young and needlessly. I wish I could have remembered his name. I felt guilty for not remembering. And was it guilt for living that had overcome me for so long? Could I finally let go of the guilt?

After I left, I got in my car and drove to my father's family plot.

Like the church and school, it was built in the late eighteen hundreds. The German cemetery was part of my family. My father's family had put down roots, buying the two lots in Brooklyn with the houses and plots in the cemetery. The first to be buried from my family was a young man who had died at twenty-seven in 1895. My father, at fifty-seven, was the last to be buried here. He laid next to his mother, father, sister, aunt, and other relatives I never knew.

I pulled up to the old iron gate and parked outside it. Then I took out the letter and flowers I had bought. Before I locked the car, I hid my purse under the driver's-side seat. The woman who I spoke to over the phone for the plot information had warned me of something I already knew. "Be careful, and don't go there late in the afternoon, people get jumped. And remember to lock your car. Try not to go alone."

Her words walked with me up the path as I looked for the family plot. It was getting late. The sun, although bright, hung low in the fall sky. No one knew I was here alone, and I had wanted it that way. It was my journey to make alone and say what I never got to say to my dad.

I survived living here as a child, and so I believed I would be okay.

The cemetery was one of the oldest and most unique graveyards in Brooklyn.

My church, school, and cemetery were once a big part of the family before I was born. There was a policy I had learned after reading about the history of this cemetery and church. It was that no divisions in death between the rich and the poor were allowed. Every grave was only permitted a simple wooden or metal marker. My grandfather, who was well-off, would feed the poor during the Depression. I was proud of him for that. Somewhere along the way, we became poor and, like most, looked down on for it. It didn't matter why or how to me anymore. But for here in the cemetery, everyone was equal.

I found the gravesite.

The last time I was here I was with my mom, sisters, brother, and a few others at a simple funeral that we all chipped in for. It had been the first time I had ever seen the family plot. It felt so isolated from the rest of the world.

One well-aged copper marker that stood the test of time and this neighborhood had our last name diagonally written across the front. The marker wasn't the same as when I had first seen it. It had a big dent in the right side of it, as if someone had tried to steal it by banging on it with a pipe or metal bat to loosen it from the ground. I ran my hands along the raised metal letters of the headstone, then examined the damage. I wondered if I could fix it. I recalled a few years back that the price of copper had skyrocketed, and when they tried to take it the headstone wouldn't budge. Its roots were as deep as the family tree.

My thoughts turned back to my dad. I could remember how he had once told me that when he died we shouldn't bring flowers or come visit him, as he wouldn't be there.

I placed the yellow carnations and pink roses down in front of the headstone and sat on the grass. The color yellow represented joyfulness, which I was feeling. Joy that I had found my new home and would move soon. Joy that I could do the work needed to emotionally grow. The carnation was the flower of mourning standing in for the grief I had felt for lost time and love that came with forgiveness and understanding for my father's pain. Something he couldn't get past. The roses were pink for gratitude and peace that I hoped he had.

"I'm sorry." I said, looking down. "I know you said not to come or bring flowers, but I know you really did like them." As I said it out loud, part of me felt as if I was defying him by being there. But then I realized he might have wanted someone to visit his grave. I could never know for sure. For me, being there felt complete. And I could remember what I learned about myself and to let go of the past and hold on to the bits that were good.

My family and dad would always be a mystery to me, as he gave little away about himself, only the stories of his childhood in Brooklyn. Now I had my own story to tell.

Taking in the moment, I opened the letter and read it out loud. Crying and stumbling over the words I had always hoped to say when he was alive. Then I told him of the place I found and how he would have loved it. I finished with *I love you*. The words I had always hoped he would say to me and that I could have said to him when he was alive. After sealing the letter, I buried it under the headstone and walked away toward a new beginning. One I was sure my dad would have been proud of and would have loved for himself.

CHAPTER 20:

FIT FOR A RAMBLER

After ten years in the carriage house and my trip to Yellowstone with Melissa, I knew I had to move. But I wanted to start my new life with a clean slate. Going back to the place I was born, I had made peace with the past.

When I went searching for a new home in Upstate New York, it didn't take long to find my dream house and way of life. A friend and horse lover told me about a town that she thought I would like. She competed there for hunter/jumper shows. After going online to check it out, I set up with a real estate agent to look at half a dozen houses. I was working on instinct, and it said the first pair was a no go.

But when we turned down the winding country road to see the third house, my heart raced. As we past a red barn and open fields and even before I saw the house, I got goosebumps. Every turn was like déjà vu. It was as if I was heading home to a place I had lived before in another lifetime. Or was it some parallel world I was crossing over to? Everything was familiar. I knew, as I knew with the carriage house, that this was home. But unlike the carriage house, it was the first time in my life I had truly felt I was home. A home that had lived in my heart forever. It was a place I'd dreamt of as a child. A place I felt I belonged.

Knowing nothing else about the town, I took a leap of faith. Leaving my Long Island horse farm for a country home I nicknamed the "Tree House," I was ready to start a new way of living.

It was a three-story brown house in the woods with a pond and stone wall, and it was perfect for the person I had become. It had a long-forgotten logging road that would take me further into the wilds of Upstate New York and myself.

The day I signed the papers and started moving into the house, a peregrine falcon flew over my head. That bird had shown up so many times before at meaningful point in my life.

The peregrine falcon as a spiritual guide is about taking action and leveraging an opportunity without overanalyzing, something I had done too much of in the past.

But not anymore. I had trusted my instincts, and the sign of the falcon was confirmation.

The hippy town of Woodstock was only a short drive away. There I found mystics, musicians, clairvoyants, artists, and card readers—my kind of people. Some became new friends, art collectors, animal lovers, and hunters.

It was there that I learned about empathies. After I read about it, it made perfect sense. I understood why I was so good at connecting with animals and why I hurt for everyone in pain around me. Whether emotional or physical, I would feel it. Now I would work on separating my own feelings from someone else's. This would take time.

After renewing my wildlife rehabilitator's license, I became flooded with phone calls. Most required nothing but information on the local wildlife. Others called about wildlife, such as foxes and skunks, making homes too close to a human house. The rest were of dogs and cats attacking a nest and causing injuries. One such call came close to home, only a few miles from my house on a farm.

When I stepped out of my truck, the air smelled of fresh-cut grass and sweet honeysuckle. It brought me to the first day at the nature center where I trained to be a wildlife rehabilitator. I smiled at the memory, though that happy look faded when I caught something moving at the edge of the field. With good peripheral vision, I could see it was a doe. She stood a few feet away at the tree line. But it was more than that. I could feel her. I knew who she was and why she was there by her stiff body. I felt her worries and helplessness, her pain.

When I looked in her direction, she stamped her foot at me. She was the mother of the fawn I was coming to collect. The fawn the farmer found hanging from a fence. I was sure of it. I could feel the doe watching me as I walked up to the farmer. Her agony made my stomach knot up—a revelation for me. To know the reason why I had always felt everything so deeply calmed my being. Now I could begin to separate my feelings from the feelings of others. It'd been a long time coming. It was also a lesson I still had to actively practice. Because I wanted to take on everyone's problems, sometimes to my own demise.

"Hey, hello," I said and gave a quick smile, holding out my hand to the farmer. "I'm Jo, the rehabilitator. I'm here for the fawn."

"Okay. I have it in the crate over here." As he walked me over, he added, "I found it hanging from a fence. I heard her call for over an hour."

He pointed to the barbwire fence up the hill. I looked up to where he pointed. The hillside was lush and green, yet it felt unnatural. It was the sharp barbwire fence that bothered me. Was it put up to divide the land? Regardless, it was like cars speeding by, something evolution didn't explain to the doe and her fawn.

The farmer's dog, medium sized with floppy ears and no pedigree, followed us up to where the fawn was.

"The dog must have found it hiding in the field and then chased it when it ran."

I imagined the fawn running, terrified, thinking the dog was a hungry coyote. She could outrun and hide from the coyote-dog but not the snarl of the wire.

I could feel the farmer's pangs of regret and see it in his frown. Was he regretting not investigating sooner? He hunched his shoulders and pursed lips as his voiced strained.

As we walked up to the house, in almost a whisper he continued to tell me the story of how he had found the fawn.

"It sounded like a human baby. I had a one-year-old, and it sounded like her."

I couldn't help but wonder why he would wait so long to investigate. Especially if it sounded so much like a child.

A few steps ahead of me, the dog's demeanor was the opposite of the farmer. As the farmer held his head down, his dog held her tail up high, proud of her prizes.

I had gotten so many calls about cats and dogs killing or maiming wildlife but didn't tell the farmer that. I could see he already felt bad. He walked me over to the small pet carrier sitting in the grass.

"I guess the dog was chasing it," he said again, never making eye contact with me.

Peaking in the crate, I could see the fawn was less than a week old. I imagined her hanging upside down from a barbwire fence. She was silent now. I could almost hear the echoes of her crying, calling for her mother with a long, terrified, mournful *mom-mom-mm-mom-mom*.

Once, right after I moved, I was driving to the store and a saw a small fawn laying on the side of the road. I pulled over to find that she was dying. There was nothing I could do to help her. So I stayed with her until she passed. I ran my hand over her head and held her, whispering softly to her. I said I was so sorry for her pain and that I would stay with her till the end. She passed in my arms as tears ran down my face. I felt so helpless.

It hurt my heart to imagine the struggle this fawn had gone through now. So new to this world, it made me think of children and how precious and abused some are. Wanting, trusting, waiting for love, for comfort. Only to be given fear and pain. I felt that's what it was like for the wild ones. I would think of them as children of the earth, and humans could either be one with them or their worst nightmares.

I didn't want to talk anymore and instead wanted to leave, as it had become overwhelming to know that the fawn's mother was watching.

I nodded as the farmer spoke but was only half listening as we walked back to my truck. I picked up the pet carrier and loaded it into the back of the jeep.

"Well, thank you for calling. I'll let you know how she's doing in a few days and drop off the carrier."

"No, no," he said, shaking his head. "You can keep the carrier."

"Okay. Thank you."

I felt purposeful to be able to help, yet guilty and in anguish for what this mother and child were going through.

On the drive home, I had flashbacks of my own fears as a new mother, an old pain of feeling helpless. It was when Melissa was only two weeks old. She had a fever and cried in a way I had never heard before. I rushed her to the hospital. She was sick with spinal meningitis and had to be hospitalized in the ICU. My child's life was in jeopardy. My heart pounded faster as I considered my worst fear—that I could lose the baby I had just given birth to and loved so deeply. It was an unbearable time, my baby in the ICU with an IV in her little head.

I shook the memories away. Then I hoped I had caught the doe's eyes and that she had felt my great desire to help her baby. This was the part that made me excited and that I worked so hard for. I had to be careful with my money, as work and sales were sometimes scarce, and raising a fawn wasn't cheap. It was rare when someone would help by buying the goat's milk or paying for a vet visit.

Back at the house, I opened the crate and took out a small fawn, not more than a few days old. She didn't move or protest. Her back leg was dug into deep by the barbwire. I was afraid for her. She looked exhausted. After I cleaned her leg, I looked into her eyes. It made me want to cry. And it was then that I fell in love.

After I cleaned her leg, I put her in a closet that I had set up with blankets. It was a warm place to rest in quieted darkness. I was lucky, as my friend Nancy was at the horse show in town that week. I called my horse-vet friend, and she said she would come over the next day. She had an X-ray machine in her truck and gave me antibiotics.

Bella, the little fawn with big helpless eyes, tugged at my core.

A few days later, I thought she should get some fresh air and be around familiar sounds, so I set up a pen outside. She couldn't stand but for a moment or two. Yet she looked content to be in familiar surroundings.

Then she went into my art studio—a two-car garage. I took out the old doors and put French glass doors in their place. It had a magnificent view with northern exposure. I placed the pen so I could watch her as I worked.

I turned away for a moment to my painting, then looked back in astonishment. The fawn's mother was nose to nose with the baby.

She had found her!

"Ow my god, she found her!" I said. I jumped up excitedly, but then stepped slowly out the door and spoke in soft tones to not scare her away. "Hey, Momma, you found your baby. She's going to be all right, I promise."

Her ears twitched as she listened. I told her how I was sorry that this had happened. And that Bella would need to stay with me for a while until she healed.

Bella means beautiful in Italian. And named after Stella, which was *star* in Italian and what I called my Stella—my little Stella Bella. It seemed that this fawn was the reincarnation of my beloved Stella. A beautiful star. It was in her sweet personality and the way she moved.

The doe looked at her baby one more time before walking away. Bella called for her, but she only turned to look, then kept walking. Every day after, I put Bella out for a short while at the same time in the afternoon, and her mother would come back and visit. Even though the doe milk had dried up, and Bella couldn't stand for long, I had a thought. What if the doe and I could work together to raise Bella?

Respecting their time together, I sat close but far enough away not to make her nervous.

As the days passed, I became part of the family.

One day, a neighbor walked up the road to go mushroom hunting and saw Bella in the pen with her mother and me close by.

"Hey there," he said. "Can I see the fawn?"

Bella's mother stamped her feet and huffed at him.

"I'm so sorry, but it's not a good idea. That's her mother." I gestured to the doe. "She comes to visit every day, and I guess she's being protective. Sorry."

I had been led to believe that wild animals can't tell one person from another. But that idea was changing.

I saw firsthand the complex relationships wild families had with each other. Without always using words, I had learned to speak and understand their body language. Was I becoming bilingual in animal talk?

After I moved to my new country home, I dragged a chair next to the stone wall close to the pond. Unknown to me, there was a small hole in the ground, apparently the home of Mr. Chipmunk. He came out, and I thought he was yelling at me.

"I'm sorry," I said, looking down. "I didn't know you lived here. I'm just having my coffee and wanted to enjoy the view if that's all right with you."

I was ready to move my chair away. But he surprised me when he disappeared down the hole, then came back up with a nut and sat and ate while I drank my coffee.

We would meet at that spot every day for the longest time.

I took long walks in the woods and stayed up until four, sometimes five in the morning to see the sunrise. In the afternoon I would sit next to the hummingbird feeder on the deck. I wanted to paint the male, ruby-throated hummingbird. He stunned me by sitting on my hand, then the females would fly around my head and pull my hair.

Outside my bedroom window was a tall, old hickory tree. To my delight, there were mourning doves nested there, just like they used to do on the horse farm before they cut down the trees. Was this some strange coincidence?

Before I had moved to the Tree House, I found a white-and-brown cocker spaniel. She had big green eyes, endless eyelashes, and acted more like a springer spaniel. She was perfect for a life in the woods. She was so smart and pretty that a friend and animal-actor agent got Jessy some great gigs. Now Jessy was an actress and model and new nanny to the wildlife. She loved the attention and worked in a film and did ads for GAP and magazines ads. But her favorite role was being a nanny for Bella and some of the other critters that came into our life.

Jessy sat with Bella and me in the studio, and I sculpted her, then cast her likeness in bronze.

After I finished her sculpture, she sniffed it and gave me a wag of approval.

After that, anytime I sculpted other animals, she looked confused about why it didn't look like her.

All this was wonderful, and I was loving every minute.

Yet it was Bella who I had felt closest to.

I was raising an eastern cottontail I named Hercules the same time as I had Bella. They both lived in the studio while I was working on an outdoor enclosure for Bella.

When I let Hercules go, he made a home in the woodpile, like Chi-Chi had years ago. I would go outside and call for Bella, who most of the time came right back, but if she didn't, I would ask Hercules. Hercules would sit up and sniff the air and turn as if to point in a particular direction. If I went the way Hercules said with his twining nose, I would always find Bella.

In late spring I'd sit by the pond. It was a morning nature meditation. A rhythm revealed itself like a hook to a song and reminded me of playing double Dutch as a child. I wanted to see if I could stay in that rhythm, like when we'd danced within the twirling jump ropes. Taking in the sight and sounds, the songs of redwing blackbirds and spring peepers and the scent of a freshly laid nest of turtle eggs. I had become as familiar to them as they were to me, and the turtles would follow my canoe whenever I went. There was a white birch alone on the edge of the pond, reminding me of when I stood alone in this world. I no longer felt that way.

I learned how to forage for wild mushrooms and berries. I removed invasive species of plants from my property.

Sharing the land and food with the bears and birds, I cultivated wild raspberries. They soon grew aplenty, as did the milkweed for the monarch butterflies.

I had created a certified wildlife sanctuary. During hunting season, deer and turkeys would spend their time napping and eating. They would rase their young here.

This new life stilled my mind and the nightmares. The ones that had haunted me for so long gave way to a dream of rebuilding the house in Brooklyn. The house that no longer existed, except in my mind. And the little girl who died a thousand deaths there knew I would always hold and protect her. Sometimes on rare occasions I would awaken in blackness. Maybe because of a deep memory that never revealed itself for the pain. Yet I still felt the same. But it was only a small lingering smoke of a forgotten life.

When I have that dream it leaves me melancholy for an hour or a day, and I allow it to be, as my grieving for that little girl has ended, though she will always be with me. I take her on my walks. She's next to me in the forest. She glides in the pond in wonder of this world and all its diversity of life. I see through her eyes, and it brings me joy.

Other joys in my life were to help the sanctuaries that relied on fundraising. Every year I would pick a cause, and that year I had been working with a wolf sanctuary, painting their star wolf I would donate for a fundraiser. They had chosen the wolf because they were being persecuted in the wild. It was after I watched a documentary on Yellowstone and how wolves were such an important part of the ecosystem.

I was also hand painting a couple dozen prints of the wolf for the gala fundraiser held at Richard Gere's new restaurant. I had met him before at another fundraiser.

Bella's first night alone in the woods was hard to cope with as she ran off in a lightning storm. The moonlight only lit up the dark so much, and it wasn't enough for my eyes to find her. I called and cried in fear for her, as the bear and coyotes had been around. Chilled to the bone and exhausted, I gave up around three am and went to bed—but not for long.

I knew deer dealt with the weather every day in nature, but Bella was still small and limped and would be easy prey. I spent the rest of the night alone in the woods or looking out the window for her. I must have passed out and around six AM when I heard her calling for me: *Ma-aa! Ma-aa!*

I jumped up and ran to the window. The fresh summer rain still on the ground, her looking up at me, tail wagging with her *Ma, I'm hungry* call.

"Thank God!" I yelled as I ran for the door, shouting, "She's here!" Jessy was right behind me crying for her, then covered her with dog saliva. After her bottle, Bella covered her with fawn kisses.

I went to the wolf gala the next evening feeling exhausted but excited, as we had an artic wolf there that I had done a portrait of. And

Helene Grimaud, a well-known French classical pianist, gave a recital. Richard Gere and his family showed up. I asked Mr. Gere for a brief interview, and he was nice enough to accommodate me. He was humble and sweet to host the party for the wolves, and I found him to be a true nature lover. I thanked him for hosting the fundraiser and gave his family a hand-painted print of a wolf.

I went home elated and spent the evening with Bella, feeling a little guilty for having just hung out with a wolf.

Shortly after that night, and just before I moved Bella out to her new enclosure, I had a strange dream that felt so real. I was in a supermarket standing in the produce department. I was thinking of how strange it felt to be there in the middle of the night and why I'd be shopping so late. Then Bella appeared, and it felt as if she belonged there.

She ran to me, calling me, tail wagging, nose up, sniffing the air.

Next, she was at my side, nudging me, then circling the cart.

I woke abruptly, saying her name. It must have been about two AM, and I felt a pinch of panic. I needed to check on her. Sometimes I did this late at night when I couldn't sleep, and she would be curled up and peek her sleepy head to say, "What, Mom?"

But when I ran downstairs to check on her, she was up and pacing. Was she hungry? Did she enter my dreams, or was it something in me that felt that she needed me at that moment? She hadn't missed a bottle, and there was no accounting for it, as she never did it again.

Had I come so far that I was connecting to myself and nature? Was this really possible?

The next week, I moved Bella outside in a "soft release," slowly weaning her.

Bella would spend the mornings with me and the afternoons with her mother. The doe would appear on the edge of the forest with another doe and fawn. I threw my head back, as this was our greeting to each other. She did the same. I would tell Bella to go, and she would leave with them. In the late afternoon, her mother would bring her back to me, and I'd nod to her, pet Bella, and take her home. I fed Bella and kept her safe. But I could never do what her mother could and that was show her the ancient trails of her wild ancestors. If she was near, I felt her before ever seeing her. I would sometimes only have to think of her and she would appear.

As she grew, we would all take long walks in the woods. I became a rambler of the wild, and the wildlife accepted me as one of theirs. It was Bella's doing, as she would bring her deer friends around. She would keep her babies close to the woman who lived in the Tree House in the woods.

I learned so much about life from Bella. There are so many kinds of love, and the heart has no boundaries. Bella would always walk with a slight limp. A handicap, something I shared.

Yet the mind and spirt can be a force more willful than the body. It can be the start of new beginnings.

CHAPTER 21:

WILD ANIMALS

A s I awoke, a soft voice whispered in my head. It grew louder as I rose to look out my window. It said, *Go wander through the woods.*

My adventures in the forests were captivating and wonderful and the best part of my day.

After breakfast of tea and toast, I readied myself to go outside. To stave off the chill, I put on my red ski jacket, ski hat, thick black gloves, two pairs of socks, and heavy boots. As I dressed, I was also preparing my mind to be present for every moment. It had taken such practice to do so, and I likened my forest bathing to diving into an ocean wave. I would focus myself to the now as I did when working on an art project. Being in the studio in a controlled environment was easy. Out in nature, my mind would still wander away to the past or future. I was good at being in the moment, but it still required practice.

I stepped outside into the cold and took a deep breath of freezing air. A pure-white carpet of snow sparkled like diamonds. It momentarily blinded me in the morning sun.

The purpose of my outing was to find fresh tracks. I wanted to discover what other creatures were wandering about. The tracks and trails of most who lived there had become familiar. Yet there was the excitement and anticipation of a surprise discovery or visitor. It was a struggle to walk through the foot of snow. Only a few steps in, I fell and laughed.

I had now spent over two years living in the Tree House. When I walked in the snow, I still walked like a penguin going up an icy hill. But I had become a part of the wilderness. My struggles and victories weren't much different from the ones I saw around me. That comforted me and gave me the confidence to always move forward, even if I knew it would be a challenge.

My property bordered a forty-five-acre field on one side and a hundred acres of vacated farmland in the back. The farm property had abandoned cars—a VW Bug, a station wagon, and an old, rusted Ford truck. All were being swallowed by the woodlands. In the two years and four seasons I had been living in the woods, I discovered things I didn't expect to be there, like gravestones from the eighteen hundreds deep in the woods, weather-beaten and forgotten names disintegrating into the forest floor. There was a one-room stone schoolhouse with a fireplace and two half-walls still standing. It felt alive with the past energy of the children who once learned here. Stopping to rest there many times, I would let my imagination take over where I could almost see into the past and to what life must have been like here a hundred years ago.

It was remarkable how the earth took back our abandonments. The metal cars that rusted away. The wood that rotted. The stone buildings that fell back to the earth. Would these be some would-be future discoveries for archeologist to examine?

But in this time and place, it was my soul food. I could feel the life in me and all around me. And at night, it permeated my dreams. Instead of the nightmares, I now dreamt of animals, and I would sometimes fly over the trees or dream of my paintings. Once I had been working on a painting of a timber wolf in a Yellowstone setting, but there was something that didn't feel right, and it perplexed me. Then I dreamt I was standing in front of the painting, and Brad Pitt was there. He said, "It's the composition, it's all wrong." Then left. Still in the dream, I wrote him a letter thanking him for his help. When I woke I went to the studio and put gesso over my canvas and started again. Brad was right, and my wolf had his eyes.

The wild in its being, its soul-sustaining life, was free to be itself. It has a collective consciousness that I felt blessed to be a part of. That collective consciousness would speak to me when I was awake or in my dreams and during creative activities. On these beautiful days, when I was in the zone of these connections, a peacefulness would wash over me like fresh water rushing in a stream. It was something I had aspired to my whole life and had finally found it. To be one with nature taught me about myself, as the wilderness loves and knows itself well. I had gained some of its secret wisdom from this wild, free world. Still, there was more to learn beyond what my eyes could see.

Feeling a bit like a wild animal, my senses became alert to every sound and the slightest of movements as I walked. Soon I came upon an old logging road where the tree branches hung over with the weight of the snow. Slowing down, I picked though the pieces of my life like thin flakes of burnt paper, trying to find clues. Transparent words of the how and why of life that I could lift to the sunlight peeking through the trees. Yet as I did, my thoughts whisked away, replaced by the winter wonderland and the now of the moment. Leaving me wondering. I could never really know, only speculate, about the reasons for life and evolution. There had been so many me's, so many evolutions, so many for the earth and for the creatures.

Only ten minutes in, sensing something close, I looked around and spotted a black fox. I had only ever seen red ones in the wild before. It was extraordinary with a dark, furry coat and bold, white chest. The tail, called the brush, was full, and he was magnificent.

He hadn't noticed me and kept walking. Then he stopped and turned to look back at me, like a breathing statue on the frozen pond. Had he sensed me there?

Motionless, I too stayed frozen in my spot but was smiling from ear to ear.

We played a game of who would move first, and I could wait for him to move on as long as he wanted, taking pictures with my mind's eye to use later on a canvas and tell his story of our moment in the woods.

Each trip out on the pond in the canoe and every walk in the woods told a story that I wanted to share with the world.

Not long after, I made a special trip to the art-supply store to find the perfect-sized canvas. Before even picking up a brush, I would stare at the canvas until I could see the painting. If I couldn't imagine it, feel it first, I couldn't start. I needed to examine what I wanted to say with my art and how I could take the viewer of the art on a journey. Where did I want them to look first? And where did I want them to rest their eyes? How did I want them to feel? What was I trying to say? This is how I connected and became my best form of communication.

But that had changed.

Back in the studio, I would paint that black fox by the stream on that 18x24 canvas, enjoying the memory with each stroke of my brush.

It also left me with more questions about that collective and our evolution.

When the snow left the ground in the late spring that year, so did the dark-eyed juncos for their summer homes.

As I sipped my tea on the deck, I saw Hercules; the eastern cotton-tail I had raised. He was grassing in the new beds of grass, clovers, and dandelions. I got up to ask where Bella was. It was always a thrill that I only had to ask him where she was, and he would sit up, sniff the air, and point me in the right direction.

Not long after, on a walk in early summer, I found Bella close to her outdoor enclosure, an out building I had fenced in for her to keep her safe before being released into the forest. It had become Bella's chosen home where she had given birth to twins. The fawns grew and played hide-and-seek and ran away when Bella came over to say hel-lo and sometimes groom me. It made me laugh and happy to watch them; they were wild and free. I was a proud deer mama to Bella, even with her slight limp, which some would call a handicap, but Bella had made it through one of the hardest winters on her own, and here she was thriving.

She wasn't the only one.

Goosey, the Canadian goose, had also become part of our wild family. He had a bit of a twisted leg and walked with a little more wad-dle than he should have. Yet every year, the day after the eggs hatched, Goosey and his wife (who I called Big Mama) would bring the new babies to the house. He would call from the bottom of the deck, and I would run to see. Then we would all go for long walks together along the pond, and I would hawk watch for them as they grazed or slept. How incredible we were as a family.

Finding my voice and loving myself for who I was took a long time. When it seemed like my wild friends did it naturally.

And it had come to me that summer when I was meeting my daughter Mellissa for lunch. We were munching down like rabbits on salads and chitchatting when the conversation got deep. It often did. I wasn't one for small talk, and neither were my girls, who had followed me to my country home and now were all grown and making their own lives.

It was then that she asked me what I would want to change about myself.

I shouldn't have been surprised, as I was always changing something. I read self-help books. Even moving the furniture around regularly. I was always working to improve my diet, my health. I was meditating, doing yoga, trying new ways of doing everything. Yet I didn't hesitate to answer her. "Nothing," I said.

I told her, "I believe in myself. I like myself just the way I am."

She went quiet. I could see the wheels turning in her head.

So, I said with a loving smile, "It took me a long time to get to the place where I could say that with confidence. I'm at peace with myself."

But I didn't even realize it till that moment. Until I said the words.

She looked startled, then replied, "You must want to change something about yourself."

I said with poise, and again with no hesitation, "No. I'm perfect right now the way I am." Then took a bite of my salad and thought for a moment. "Why can't I be? Self-improvement is great. And I always want to be my best, but not if it comes from self-loathing. I've been there and done that. I'm happy with who I am and proud of what I've accomplished."

Driving home, it had made me think about the progress I had made. It felt good to say and more important to believe it.

Progress: it's hard to see when you're living it. Just like back in college when I painted over my canvas, I became blind to it. Art school had brought to the forefront a visual picture of who I could be. Animals had reminded me of who I always was. Both had a place in my life. Creating art would allow my mind to stay in nature when my body was fatigued.

Every day I was working through the complexities of life, my own emotions, and what it all meant. This place and life made my chronic pain manageable by distracting me with its charm. But when I needed more than it could give, I had a good doctor for the bad days or weeks that were sure to come. While I still freelanced as an artist, mostly, my plan to work from home helped. I still went out on jobs when I could—on a set from local film companies or working with my dog Jessy. I did what I could. Jessy was a great actor and beautiful model and got several gigs. She loved to work and was a real people person. I was getting better at my people skills and had several galleries around the county helping me sell my work.

Yet I had missed my own art opening, a solo show at a local gallery, because I was too sick to get out of bed. Disappointed about the way things were sometimes but okay with it. What else could I do? Life gives you what it wants, and I was going to make the best of it. I had a local falconer fill in for me for the opening with some of my favorite birds of prey.

I had to keep my life simple. Even if my walk became too much, my bed was never that far away. It made me feel secure and free to be with nature.

I completed the black-fox-in-winter scene that spring and sold it in the summer. I was often working on several paintings at the same time. If I got stuck with one, I would work on something else. I thought I was done with foxes for a while.

Then that summer, while in my studio at four o'clock for an entire month, a red fox started showing up every day. He sat right outside the studio, staring at what seemed like nothing. I stopped painting and pulled out my clay and began sculpting him where he sat, listening to "Stairway to Heaven" by Led Zeppelin a hundred times on a loop. The fox didn't seem to mind me or the music. When the work was completed and Led Zeppelin was tired of singing, the fox left. Never returned at four or any other regular time. What "Stairway to Heaven" had to do with the four-o'clock fox and sculpture was a mystery. But what I knew for sure was that I was in full synchronicity with the life I had always wanted, going with the flow. A fox shows up at four, I show up, and magical things happen. That was my new motto.

The curtain had been pulled back to life in the forest, and I learned foxes can tell time.

Nature and its wild animals had let me into their lives. Was it so I could see and share their message of struggles? It was time to use that voice and speak for my loved ones in a new way. I needed to do more than paint and sculpt them, raise them and donate my art for conservation or volunteer. Becoming a local producer and public speaker was my answer and new challenge. It was the way I would push myself to do more. It was uncomfortable, but I was ready for it.

A thought turned to an action, and a few months later it was standing-room only at the wolf center where I went to speak. My throat was dry, and my palms were sweaty as I waited in the doorway to go up and tell the stories of my wild encounters.

What was I thinking? I wanted to run, but then I couldn't help but remember how I would hide behind the door as a child when strangers came over. Nor could I forget the time in college in my first-year writing class when we all had to get up in front of the class and read our stories out loud. After class, I went to speak to my professor. He was a stiff man who was emotionally immoveable. I had begged and even cried to him, "Please, I can't do it. I have a fear of talking in front of people. There must be some other way. I'm happy to do extra work."

"No," he said without an ounce of sympatry. "You'll fail if you don't do it."

The next day in class, as I walked up to the front, a piece of paper in my shaking hands, my throat became a desert of dryness. It was still that way now every time I spoke to a crowd or at an art opening. It had felt like I was going to pass out. Reading my story that first time in front of the class in college over twenty-five years ago was horrific. I stumbled over the words, and my face became so red that I felt my ears pulsing.

But I did it.

Now, with my wildlife art displayed around me and my slide presentation set up, I walked to the front of a room to speak. My nerves disbursed as I talked about my wild family and how I had learned to communicate and connect with them. After the talk, people hung around to share their stories or encounters. One woman wanted to get her wildlife-rehabilitation license and asked if I could help her learn.

"That's amazing," I said. "There's such a need for help."

Then I took classes and became certified as a local television producer. I was going to have my first show about wolves at a new, state-of-the-art television studio ten minutes from my house. How lucky was I!

"Is it okay to bring a wolf to the set for an interview?" I asked the director of the local cable studio.

"A *real* wolf?" She sounded confused.

"Yes, a real wolf. An ambassador wolf. A white arctic wolf. A photographer who published a book on wolves too. The show is about wolves and why we need them in the wild."

"Oh." She hesitated. "We never had one on or such a request before. I'll have to check."

She called me back a few days later, and we did the show. I loved every minute. It felt great to help share what I had learned.

But the real "I-have-arrived" moment came when I asked Jim Fowler for an interview. I'd worked with him for well over ten years, but he was always busy, and it was a big ask. To my amazement, he said yes!

"You know, JoAnne," Jim said in his deep, knowing voice, "you should get a sponsor."

"Okay, Jim. But I'm not sure how to do that."

Putting a volunteer team of four together for the interview was easy. I needed a sound man, a cameraman, a photographer, and a tech person. All I had to say was that I was interviewing Jim Fowler at his home in Connecticut. The response went like this: "Jim Fowler? He's great, love watching him. I'm in."

I met my friend Bobby, who I was proud to say was an Emmy-winning cameraman, on the set of the *Martha Stewart Show*. He had also worked at Channel 13 for most of his career. He had filmed celebrities and presidents. How lucky was I to have him as my cameramen and art collector. He helped me when I interviewed Richard Gere and Bobby Kennedy and now Jim Fowler. He filmed my paintings. My girlfriend from college was my photographer with two others from the studio. They were all enamored and said they felt like kids being around Jim.

I had all my questions on flashcards so as to not forget all the things I wanted to know about him.

We sat down by his pond. Then it happened. It was the little girl in me who spoke. I was having a flashback right then. I could see myself—belly down, holding up my chin on the floor, watching Jim in the wild and on talk shows with animals.

I felt like I was five years old.

Somewhere in the middle of the interview I felt I had to tell Jim the truth about me. Something in all the years that I knew him I had never mentioned. In the past we had talked about our children and the show we were doing and animals, but I'd never told him what I wanted to tell him. It went something like this: "Jim, you know, I grew up in the ghetto. And, you see, your show was one of the shows that helped me get through that difficult time in my life. It helped me want to help animals too. Seeing you on TV made me want to do more with my life and in a way helped save me."

I could see the surprise on his face. And I can't remember exactly what he said, but he looked me in the eye and said something like, "That's tough. That's a different kind of jungle—a different kind of wildlife."

"It was," I said. "But seeing you on the television made it easier and gave me something to look forward to."

After it was over, I felt like I had just left a dream that I could never have imagined would come. I almost felt like I had to pinch myself to believe this was happening. As I asked my questions and we talked, I could see smiles on everyone around, enjoying it as much as I was.

When we finished, we packed up and piled into the car. We drove in silence, all in our own heads, entranced by Jim and what we had just gotten to do. For me, it was more that I had finally freed myself of the shame of where I grew up. I no longer hid behind a door in the closet.

It was s okay that I couldn't spell and liked to stay up late and sleep in. It was okay to be me, a girl who had grown up in the ghetto. And now I could be fearless. I would never let anyone judge me, nor would I judge myself for things I couldn't control, like where and how I grew up. I could be proud of who I was and what I'd become. Maybe there was a reason for my experiences, to share how precious being in and around nature is to one's soul.

It seemed to me as I drove home that day that all my childhood dreams had come true.

Wanting to be a superhero—I had become one to the wild-animal babies that grew strong and went back to the wild to be free and live a full life.

I wanted to live in the country, and here I was. Speaking their language like Dr. Doolittle did with the animals wasn't a dream anymore.

Art somehow found me. When I was lost about who I was, it freed me, and I would always be beholden to it for bringing me to my true love of nature.

Now I had become like the wild animals around me, showing my full self and not holding back who I was anymore. It was sort of like being naked and letting your voice be heard.

Chapter 22:

Evolution Observed

I t was New Year's Eve, the cusp of a new beginning, and I was sitting in a restaurant waiting for my sandwich and soup. There was a nice couple sitting next to me also eating a soup and sandwich. Middle-aged, well-dressed. I looked around the crowded room and observed.

It's what I do as an artist.

As a lifetime habit it has served me well.

The restaurant was busy, and my order took much longer than I had expected. When the waiter came over to apologize, I said it was okay, then nicely asked, "Will it be much longer? I'm expected somewhere."

Moments later the man sitting with the woman next to me asked if I lived in the area. "I live in the next town," I replied, then asked if they lived in the area too, since it had become a high tourist location, one never knew.

The couple smiled and nodded, then the man said, "I ask because I was wondering if you were a therapist. I'm in need of a therapist." He glanced at the woman to confirm this, then turned back to me.

I smiled and gave him my full attention. "No," I said.

I waited a moment, my curiosity peaked. It seems to me that people rush to talk, and it's an art and a delicate balance to learn to listen and wait. Waiting too long to respond could create an uncomfortable silence. Not for me, of course, as I still treasure the moments of silence in between the conversation. Animals always speak the most in silence.

He continued. "I only ask because you've been sitting here for a long time, and I look at you and think, there's a woman who's calm, centered, and confident. And I thought to myself this woman seems like she has it together. She must be a therapist."

It was far from the truth of my journey to get here, but it was the truth of now. I was calm, centered, confident, and never in a hurry.

My heart warmed, and it wasn't the first time, nor do I doubt it will be the last, that people talk to me or ask for advice.

I took a breath and let the kindness of his words warm my heart and sent it back to them. I knew they felt it by their body language and the way they shifted. It was confirmed by what he said next.

"Since you've been sitting here we've felt your warm, calm energy." He spoke as if he was speaking for both of them, as if they were one.

She nodded in agreement.

I chuckled in shyness, something that's never left me, even though I can appear bold. It was a childish giggle and a bit of an embarrassment for the observation.

I felt his unspoken need for advice and trusted that instinct. At times people have asked me for my opinion or advice, but I've not given it because it didn't feel right.

But this felt different. This man was reaching out, and something guided me.

I leaned forward to tell him the truth of myself and of the nature I loved so much. I've grown to love my own freedom of honesty and enjoyment for this world, people, and animals. I spoke as if I was telling them a secret.

I said, "I did at one time, when I was young, want to be a social worker. Then I was going to join the Red Cross and travel the world. But life had other plans for me. I'm an artist, and I work with animals." I paused, then said, I don't know why you need a therapist. You live here in this beautiful place. Isn't nature around you? It's calm, peaceful, and balanced."

His smile said he agreed, and he leaned forward to listen.

I leaned even closer and said, "You could start just by breathing slow and thoughtful. Take a walk in the woods or just look out your window and be in the moment. I'm sure you have a beautiful view."

He nodded. He and his companion listened with interest.

So, I continued as if guided by an unseen force. It was as if my mouth was painting the words, just like the times my hand and brush took over, and I disappeared into some muse of being. "If you put your hand on a tree you can feel the tree is just being. It doesn't think about the past or its plans for the future, it always lives fully in the moment."

I paused, then shared some small snippets of my stories and what I'd learned from my beautiful wild family. I wanted them to see and think differently of the deer and the forest just outside their window or while on a walk. I sought to share some of what it was like for them living in our world.

What I hoped for now was for people to know the joy that I felt living in the moment of gratitude of the natural world.

My food came at that time and so did a couple to take my place at the counter.

I said it was a pleasure meeting them and left feeling as if I had done something important for someone I would probably never meet again.

We all go through an evolution of the heart.

With the hundred or so lives we live in one lifetime, from birth to the grave, we go deep into the jungle of our beings. We do it better than a cat with only nine lives. We're all on a quest to find something. It's like the word on the tip of your tongue that you know you know but can't say. We're born with it. Your heart knows what it wants to be. Whether you walk on two legs, four, fly, or swim. Be it a tree or a flower. We all want to live.

My evolution was a revolution and freed me from living in the pain of a dusty past. I did so many things I wanted to. Being an artist is not for the weak at heart. I don't always have a lot of money in my pocket, but what I have is worth so much more. Love, gratitude, and a deep joy for life.

I did and still do talk to the animals, and now even the plants and trees, and they always talk back in their own special way.

"The continued existence of wildlife and wilderness is important to the quality of life of humans. Our challenge for the future is that we realize we are very much a part of the Earth's ecosystem, and we must learn to respect and live according to the basic biological laws of nature."

- Jim Fowler

About the drawings in the book:

They were picked for their relevance to the stories in the book and are from the private sketchbook journals of the author and have never been shown publicly before.

To learn more about the author's artwork and some of the other animal stories,

please go to: https://joannesullam.com

DayDreams Studio Press